The Oligarch

James Sherry

The Oligarch

Rewriting Machiavelli's *The Prince* for Our Time

James Sherry
New York, New York
USA

ISBN 978-3-319-62168-5   ISBN 978-3-319-62169-2 (eBook)
DOI 10.1007/978-3-319-62169-2

Library of Congress Control Number: 2017948163

© The Editor(s) (if applicable) and The Author(s) 2018
This work is subject to copyright. All rights are solely and exclusively licensed by the Publisher, whether the whole or part of the material is concerned, specifically the rights of translation, reprinting, reuse of illustrations, recitation, broadcasting, reproduction on microfilms or in any other physical way, and transmission or information storage and retrieval, electronic adaptation, computer software, or by similar or dissimilar methodology now known or hereafter developed.
The use of general descriptive names, registered names, trademarks, service marks, etc. in this publication does not imply, even in the absence of a specific statement, that such names are exempt from the relevant protective laws and regulations and therefore free for general use.
The publisher, the authors and the editors are safe to assume that the advice and information in this book are believed to be true and accurate at the date of publication. Neither the publisher nor the authors or the editors give a warranty, express or implied, with respect to the material contained herein or for any errors or omissions that may have been made. The publisher remains neutral with regard to jurisdictional claims in published maps and institutional affiliations.

Cover image © Antonio M. Rosario / Getty Images
Cover design by Fatima Jamadar

Printed on acid-free paper

This Palgrave Macmillan imprint is published by Springer Nature
The registered company is Springer International Publishing AG
The registered company address is: Gewerbestrasse 11, 6330 Cham, Switzerland

To the excellent Elon Musk:
Anyone who hopes to gain the favor of an oligarch offers what they think influential people enjoy. Supplicants present ostentatious building plans, brilliant patent filings, and expensive gifts such as cars, paintings, and baseball cards.

Although lacking the capital for such a princely offering, I am keen to bestow some proof of my appreciation. Thus, I present this treatise on the networks of power that I have written after years studying technology, finance, environment, and language.

These reflections, channeled through a work of great antiquity and importance, Niccoló Machiavelli's The Prince, *remind us of the timeliness and timelessness of the subject of leadership by small groups. Some of the perspectives herein may contradict conventional wisdom, but I ask you to keep an open mind.*

Though I consider this book barely worth your attention, I trust that you will be kind enough to accept it. The best gift I can offer is the opportunity to understand in the shortest time what I have learned through years of anguish and compromise, weathering the ubiquitous clamor and assault of disinformation.

Productive and effective people consider their relationships from many points of view and do not act on essential truths. Filmmakers photograph mountains from the plains, and in order to screen the plains, shoot from the peaks. There is no privileged position of comprehension. Diverse evidence must be correlated.

Take then, this little gift in the spirit that I offer it. If you consider it, it will become apparent how to reach the prominence promised by your skill, focus, and good fortune. And if, Elon, from your mountaintop, you sometimes turn your eyes to these lower regions, you will see how much your work means to the world.

Yours truly,
James Sherry

Acknowledgements

Thanks to W. K. Marriott and Jonathan Bennett whose original translations of *The Prince* formed the basis of this text.

Thanks to Jeffrey A. Winters for his book *Oligarchy* and to Gaetano Mosca and the Italian School of Elitists from which I have also freely appropriated.

And thanks to Anna Soci, Giovanni Giorgini, Kit Robinson, Michael Ruby, Dan Gross, John Reed, and Deborah Thomas for their careful reading and suggestions.

Contents

1: On the Types of Oligarchies   1
Chapter I: *How Many Forms of Governance There Are and How They Operate*   1
Chapter II: *Concerning Oligarchies Transmitted by Tradition, Inheritance, or Law*   3
Chapter III: *Concerning Mixed Oligarchies*   8
Chapter IV: *Why the Religious Oligarchs of Iran, Subjugated by the US, Rebelled Against Reza Shah Pahlavi, Forcing His Abdication, and Why Such Was Not the Case in Ukraine*   17

2: On the Details of Acquisition and Management of Organizations   23
Chapter V: *Concerning the Way to Govern Firms and States That Are Accustomed to Operate Under Their Own (By-)Laws*   23
Chapter VI: *Concerning New Oligarchies Acquired by Skill*   26
Chapter VII: *Concerning New Oligarchies Acquired Either by the Arms of Others or by Good Fortune*   31
Chapter VIII: *Concerning Those Who Have Risen to the Oligarchy by Wickedness*   34

3: Regarding the Form of Oligarchies 41
Chapter IX: Concerning a Civil Oligarchy 41
Chapter X: Concerning the Ways That the Strength of Oligarchies Ought to Be Measured 50
Chapter XI: Concerning Ecclesiastical Oligarchies 54

4: On Managing Assets within Organizations 61
Chapter XII: How Many Kinds of Assets, Workers, and Soldiery There Are, and Concerning Consultants and Lobbyists 61
Chapter XIII: Concerning Auxiliaries or Foreign Troops and Assets, and One's Own 68
Chapter XIV: That Which Concerns the Oligarch on the Subject of the Art of Finance 73

5: Guidance on Oligarchic Comportment 81
Chapter XV: Concerning Things for Which All People, and Especially Oligarchs, Are Praised or Blamed 81
Chapter XVI: Concerning Liberality and Parsimony 85
Chapter XVII: Concerning Cruelty and Clemency, and Whether It Is Better to Be Loved Than Feared 89
Chapter XVIII: Concerning the Way in Which Oligarchs Should Keep Faith 94
Chapter XIX: That One Should Avoid Being Despised and Hated 101

6: On the Projects of Oligarchs 109
Chapter XX: Are Building Programs, Walls, Fortresses, and Other Projects to Which Oligarchs Often Resort Advantageous or Burdensome? 109

7: Regarding Good Offices 121
Chapter XXI: How an Oligarch Should Conduct Himself in Order to Gain Renown 121
Chapter XXII: Concerning the Administrators of Oligarchy 132
Chapter XXIII: How Flatterers Should Be Avoided 135

8: On Risk Management and Marketplace Mentality   143
*Chapter XXIV: Oligarchs Who Have Lost Control of Their
Organizations and Networks*   143
*Chapter XXV: What Probability Can Effect in Human Affairs, and
How to Manage It*   146
*Chapter XXVI: An Exhortation to Liberate Nations and Their Citizens
from Marketplace Mentality*   152

Note on Definitions   157

1: On the Types of Oligarchies

CHAPTER I: HOW MANY FORMS OF GOVERNANCE THERE ARE AND HOW THEY OPERATE

All states and all companies that rule and have ever ruled function and have functioned as oligarchies. While there are multiple forms of governance such as republics, principalities, and corporations, all operate through control by a few.

Oligarchies are transmitted either by tradition, inheritance, or law, or they are new. In most cases, they are organized by agreement about principles and based on individual merit, but sometimes oligarchic power is inherited.

New oligarchies are either entirely new, as the United States of America was for Alexander Hamilton, Thomas Jefferson, and James Madison, or they are created from established states and companies, as in the case of the European Union, pillared on trade and banking.

Some oligarchies operate through the illusions of autocratic form as in Russia, where President Vladimir Putin's prominence conceals the cadre of oligarchs that runs the state and the economy. Other oligarchies live with the delusions of democracy as in the US, where the people have little control over their economic, political, and cultural fate, yet they insist they are free. In Russia, oligarchs use the autocracy to control and sequester financial and hard assets. In the US, oligarchs establish freedom of action for themselves to accumulate assets and control institutional processes. Freedom for the people means something quite different, as you well know.

Oligarchies in modern times are acquired either through the arms of defense industries, as in Europe after World War II; by the manipulation of popular uprisings, as with China and the Soviet Union; or by a supportive external oligarchy, as in Chile via the US-backed assassination of Salvador Allende, or in Iraq via the toppling of Saddam Hussein.

The forms of governance have received the detailed attention of political writers from Plato and Aristotle to Machiavelli and Montesquieu to Karl Marx and Thorstein Veblen, as well as through the theory of corporations, the media, and contemporary political cant. Operations, on the other hand, are obscured by immense detail and secrecy. These operational details, as much as form, regulate individual well-being. Operational skills determine individual and group successes. How political leaders operate within the form of government determines their ability to hold office and avoid unnecessary conflict. How corporate leaders operate a firm determines its profitability.

Rather than provoke a conflict in defense of form, which we all value, this book focuses on the networks of leadership that link form and operations. The driving forces behind visible leaders are these oligarchic networks that support presidents and CEOs in top administrative positions. Leadership is layered and not based on that cult of individuals that culture promotes.

Gaining support from the people requires formal consent and general consensus. Consent of the governed has been accomplished in modern times by broadening suffrage, increasing representation in government, and disseminating effective public relations. State and corporate public relations identify coalitions whose supporters are often asked to act in a manner contrary to their self-interest. The Enlightenment ideals of freedom of the mind and action have captured the support of both the masses and the intelligentsia. But state and corporate mechanisms of control have increasingly invalidated these freedoms through operational changes that override the will of the majority of citizens and workers, allowing oligarchs to increase their share of wealth and power.

Truly, democracy usually improves the well-being of the people. Yet too little consideration has been given to how different forms of governance actually function and who benefits. And it is on the other side of this scrim of form that power is wielded throughout the world.

Chapter II: Concerning Oligarchies Transmitted by Tradition, Inheritance, or Law

Republics, autocracies, and public and private companies operate similarly through control by small groups, the differences being their form, public face, and how surplus is distributed. Form alone does not determine the value of a state or corporation. Democracies impoverish their people nearly as often as autocratic forms of government and do not guarantee individual happiness and security. Zimbabwe, Haiti, and India are examples of different governmental forms of notably inequitable states in which large swaths of people suffer unnecessarily due to the uneven distribution of wealth and self-serving leadership. Singapore and Germany have healthy, productive populations in spite of differing forms.

Although the personal freedom promised by democracy usually improves individual well-being, a state government must balance economic conditions with appropriate taxation and benefits to reduce suffering and precarity among its citizens. Equality of opportunity and balancing wealth improve any organization more than too few receiving too much of either. Lower net inequality is robustly correlated with faster and more durable growth, for a given level of redistribution. If politicians and economists do not cleave too tightly to the interests of any one class, they well understand the tipping points of economic equality, after which political instability increases.

Economic power is one of the chief supports of any oligarch. You need money to pursue your programs. But the media phrase "follow the money," like vulgar Marxism, misdirects the oligarch's understanding of power by proposing a single, essential criterion for control. It creates factions among citizens and intensifies the desire for personal wealth. Looking more closely, other types of control, influence, and organization sustain power's infrastructure. Including elites—and not just the wealthy—in understanding how the few rules promotes greater accuracy about power, since the leadership network and the character of its connections, as much as wealthy individuals, shape any organization. This network continually transmits power and reroutes change throughout time and social structure, usually permitting one individual to easily replace another in leadership roles. Effective bureaucratic communications account for the longevity of certain states and cultures as much as other vectors like predictable water flows.

This network, like any complex system, operates similarly at different scales. Although the form of communications is specific to each organization, transmissions within a family or clan contain similar information to those of the corporation or state. Peace cannot be made between warring factions without go-betweens who are familiar with both sides of a dispute. Lawyers standardize methods and protect clients in commercial negotiations. Conflicts of interest are eliminated by rules developed by professional associations.

Protocols are often transformed when they pass from one entity to another or move between oligarchic groups. In Somaliland, for example, in 1999 businessmen stopped paying taxes to unreliable warlords, and transferred control of their commercial disputes to the Sharia courts of the Islamic Court Union. The ICU, made up of clan elders, businessmen, and sheikhs, derived its reliability from traditional connections to the powerful Hawiye clan of Mogadishu. This need for consistency in legal cases, especially contract law, drives oligarchs to standardize and reduce the likelihood of miscommunication. Co-location of private assets such as the endowment of the Basilica of St. Mark in Venice and offshore banking institutions such as those in the Cayman Islands and Switzerland exemplify such standards that assure oligarchs that assets are protected yet accessible to them.

The network holds sway over individuals, even the richest and strongest, and supports operations at all scales from local to global. The network's most powerful and stable nodes—both individuals and groups—tend to be those with the most connectors to other nodes, not only those with the most money or the biggest armies. Their connections are strong or weak, continuous or intermittent, mono- or bidirectional depending on conditions, but relative reliability remains vital to any channel. Hence financial transactions are matched at exchanges controlled by well-documented rules.

Highly connected individuals and groups build and defend corporations and states. Focusing only on wealthy individuals reinforces a marginal participant's desire to join these networks, acting as an incentive to join the bureaucracy. Such media focus fetishizes consumption and disguises the reins of power, since power that proclaims itself loses power. So, it is usually in the interests of an oligarch to work in the background, hence the effectiveness of oligarchs in democracies. The combined wealth and stability of civil oligarchs compares favorably to ruling oligarchs who, while potentially richer—compare the net worth of Russia's Putin to Microsoft's Bill Gates—operate at greater risk.

An oligarch finds fewer difficulties in managing states and corporations with traditional oligarchies. For example, in England, leadership was so secure it attracted much of the Venetian gold that fled its Republic prior to Napoleon's conquest in 1798. Newly minted wealth, as in Silicon Valley, is more troublesome because culture develops slowly within any domain. It takes a while for an oligarch to stabilize power relations, but it is usually sufficient to prudently address situations as they arise and avoid transgressing the customs of precursors. If a new leader like US President Jimmy Carter appears, whenever anything sinister happens to him, like an October surprise, another group ascends because culture is built around existing expectations.

The Koch brothers, Charles and David, could not have withstood the attacks of political foes if they had not been well established in the oil refineries they inherited from their father, Fred. Using that base, they sustainably diversified their holdings. They have networked conservatives for decades, building new organizations like the Cato Institute to project their power and installing their people in existing institutions like George Mason University through funding from their private foundations. They also fund the American Civil Liberties Union, prison reform efforts, and other moderate institutions that can promote aspects of libertarianism and provide suitable cover for their activities. Their network is not limited to any form of governance, but rather extends freedom of action for themselves.

The Koch brothers' notion of freedom implies that they benefit from democracy, although universal suffrage actually impedes their progress. As a result, Koch-funded organizations actively work to suppress voters in many jurisdictions. Along with other highly connected citizens like Karl Rove, lobbyist Jack Abramoff, Congressman Bob Ney, and billionaires Paul Singer and Julian Robertson, this network has, through the good offices of many Secretaries of State, like Florida's Katherine Harris and Kansas' Kris Kobach, wiped more than seven million legitimate registered voters from the rolls, mostly Democrats, students, the elderly, and people of color.

Hereditary and traditional oligarchs are unlikely to offend existing cultures. The people feel these multigenerational leaders act as they themselves have been taught to behave. In this way, all parties are apparently respected. Unless extraordinary behavior, like Howard Hughes', causes a hereditary oligarch to be mistrusted, the network will continue to support their control. Due to the duration of oligarchic hegemony, the memories and motives that drive change fade. In this way, the hereditary oligarch uses time to moderate social change.

Hereditary oligarchies, however, suffer from an inherent weakness: a scion may not have the same strength of mind or purpose as the fortune's founder. As a result, most developed nations have severely restricted the institutional guarantees of the power of inherited, aristocratic wealth. If the blood has thinned due to the chances of genetics or aesthetic training, leadership is often inherited by weaker hands. These children of oligarchs may let power slip from their grasp either by running the (e)state into the ground or by allowing it to be managed by professional administrators while they pursue their pleasure, good works, and art. If the former, then new, stronger hands will pick up the reins, and not much is lost.

But if the latter is the case, as often happens with inherited power and privilege, the (e)state is managed by lawyers and accountants—an industry that protects wealth—who have more interest in financial success than maintaining a socially responsible state or corporation. Even with the proper incentives, these professional administrators who preserve inherited wealth often promote unfair, even brutal, treatment of employees and citizens to assure profitability. The supported oligarchs, while rich beyond imagining, do not have the skills to maintain the integrity of the state or firm. The children of the Walton family appear as a fine example of disengaged, inherited wealth and power. Instead of enhancing Walmart's overall value, they allow it to be run in a way that ignores, as much as feasible, the society and infrastructure that made their wealth possible. In such cases, imbalances and inequality may become intolerable. Then the oligarchy itself becomes as vulnerable as France was in 1789 and Russia and China were in the twentieth century. Today, rising inequality, in developed countries such as the US and United Kingdom and in developing countries such as Russia and China, has begun to create imbalances and divergences—economic, political, and environmental—that suggest a turning point for humanity and a potential return of aristocratic institutional rights and privileges.

We cannot build a productive society, as highly interdependent and connected as our current world, by empowering the scions of hedge-fund managers and technology geeks. Inherited wealth can be effectively moderated by taxation, even against the efforts of the accountants and lawyers of the income protection industry. Recent studies have concluded that the equitable distribution of income is a more important contributor to sustained economic growth than openness to trade, a competitive exchange rate, level of foreign investment, or the quality and stability of a country's political institutions. Taxing inherited wealth is in the interests of all but the feckless inheritors and the hollow arguments of paternalists.

Although the US separated from Europe to avoid aristocracy, the dynamics of both society and biology make limiting dynastic aspirations difficult. Thwarting the reproduction of strong lineage remains contrary to important inherent processes, since people constantly seek to perpetuate their names and genes through their children. Even non-human interactions in animal and plant kingdoms benefit from strong individuals. Yet farsighted leaders, such as Gates and Warren Buffet, turn over the majority of their assets to the public good, while making sure their children are comfortable and encouraging them to be active. Such strategies create more stable and widely supported societies.

The people, by virtue of their numbers alone, moral considerations aside, must participate in the economies of any state for it to succeed. In China, the Qing empire, isolated from its people, allowed its economy to stagnate and fall early in the twentieth century. The impoverished populace was unable to continue to support the state. A new stable oligarchy did not arise until 1949. It remains in power today, although incursions from financialized Western influence have increased inequality in China.

When too much wealth collects in the top strata, society stagnates and the environment suffers. When society stops channeling wealth to the bottom 90 percent, who spend earnings with a 3.6 times multiplier in the economy, but instead deliver tax breaks to the top 0.1 percent, whose multiplier is fractional, it should come as no surprise that organizations fail to thrive. Then the wise oligarch must take responsibility for rebalancing rather than increasing inequality.

Financial inequality is currently increasing in civil oligarchies like the US and EU, where the people lack sufficient income to buy enough of the products that enrich oligarchs to maintain vibrant economic growth. Instead, the people become disaffected from the lack of prospects and look beyond existing networks to recapture the wealth and control they imagine they had or should have. Further isolated by unsupportive corporate cultures within identity groups, populations exhibit extreme beliefs and behaviors as in the US elections of 2016 and the Brexit vote in the UK. Recognition of this debilitating social situation by a far-sighted oligarch and well-connected groups might help stabilize and turn around societies at risk of collapse from wealth inequality and climate change driven by the oligarchs' desire for ever-greater power, wealth, and the false sense of security they offer.

Chapter III: Concerning Mixed Oligarchies

More difficulties occur in a new oligarchy because the connections of networks take time to optimize. Even when starting from a firm base, such as in the oil patch, deals must be negotiated and interests aligned, often in stressful circumstances. States and corporations based on existing institutions struggle to ally with new entities due to their vested interests and existing contracts. Prior connections fulfill the roles that the new organization seeks to occupy. Hence a new organization must offer some new operation.

Marshall Tito, for example, was able to overcome the nationalist problems of the separate Yugoslav states for nearly 40 years. But he built his network without strengthening its connections to traditional national bases of power. He jailed Catholic quislings in Croatia, cut Slovenian ties to German industry, and oppressed religious leaders in Bosnia. Although he built a strong network founded on idealism and militarism, the old networks reasserted themselves quite soon after he died.

To analyze this problem more clearly, it must be pointed out that most organizations are not purely traditional or new. At its inception in 1908, General Motors only controlled McLaughlin Car Company of Canada and Buick. Burdened by debt, founder William Durant lost control of GM to the banks in 1910. But in subsequent years, GM started Chevrolet and numerous other brands. Its network grew through World War I, the boom years of the '20s, and the Great Depression. Synergies arising from your merger of Tesla, Solar City, and battery production are still developing at the same time that each entity is struggling. Allying with the Donald Trump administration may be a useful way to balance radical influences in government as long as you maintain open channels to other power bases. Trump's affiliation with climate change deniers may, however, in the end, prevent your alliance from bearing fruit.

Maintaining power in a stagnant environment may be as difficult to control as in a changing world, as Carter discovered, since people always hope to better themselves. Candidates appeal to voters by promising, like Ronald Reagan, a new dawn, proposing little more than a return to yesterday. The past always seems better, since people forget suffering. While only the top echelons saw significant economic improvement from Reagan's "morning in America," other classes gained pride in their religions, conservative cultures, and illusions of self-reliance. Trump's slogan "make America great again" also galvanizes many voters' hope to return to an imagined past, while the Democratic Party's base is disaffected by years of stagnation and fails to connect to white working class and *petit bourgeois* voters.

CHAPTER III: CONCERNING MIXED OLIGARCHIES

When management acquires a company, some of its employees hope they'll get a better deal at the combined firm because of their loyalty. An oligarch should not disillusion them. Workers should be encouraged and middle managers reassigned. But finding the resources to enhance the firm may prove difficult because it was probably acquired for organizational synergies or cash flows, and that usually means that you need to lower expenses. Management must keep the peace, avoiding interference from prevailing internal networks and consequent reductions in productivity.

From the popular perspective, although inertia and existing affiliations play important roles in supporting organizations at all levels, throughout history people have aspired to improve their lot by overthrowing unpopular or ineffective leaders. They are often deceived in this hope, discovering that they have gone from bad to worse, or that they have simply exchanged one oligarchic regime for another. In only a few years, the revolutions in France in 1789 and in Russia in 1917 collapsed, and oligarchy returned. Change is continuous, sometimes rapid, sometimes slow; there is no continuously stable condition. Slowing change, however, to a controllable rate has proven an effective way to build a sustainable, if not impregnable, network.

To solidify control of new domains, corporations and states burden acquisitions with new contracts, taxes, and treaties. We saw this with GM after its reorganization in 2008. The government bailout allowed GM to negotiate lower wages and pensions. (The stable leadership at Ford did not need funding from new money, but the reorganized GM appears now to be the stronger of the two. Change renews despite individual suffering.)

Formerly well-paid auto workers suffered when management sought to drive down wages, citing foreign competition. Actually, competition only occurred because oligarchs' lawyers with interests in right-to-work states broke the back of unions that protected wage gains. Remember how the income protection industry shelters wealth? The publicity that supports technological innovation also masks how legal manipulations pushed wages lower. Individual workers who try to negotiate wages without a union have little leverage against an organized boardroom with professional management.

Similar pressures squeeze workers during corporate takeovers as when a new country is added to the EU. The flood of workers from the annexed organizations anger many communities in the core of existing entities be they companies or countries. New acquisitions and immigration trigger the rise of nativist fervor that may be exploited by the savvy oligarch who opens and closes borders as needed, if the courts are not united in opposition. In this way, an oligarch gains control of new pools of workers at lower wages, improving profitability of states and businesses, and then tightening borders to regain control of trade flows.

In addition to conflicts with labor, in composite oligarchies, a new network, such as technology moguls, can rise in influence to challenge and decisively sway the balance of power. The impact of computing and Internet technology on many other industries and governments is widely appreciated in capital markets, global media, and private conversation. This raises one of the other two threats to all power: competition among oligarchic groups. (The third is environmental change, which we will address later.)

As an example of competition among oligarchs, Putin was elevated to leadership by the network of ex-KGB and state industry leaders in post-Soviet Russia. He was challenged by Mikhail Khodorkovsky, owner of the oil company Yukos, who accused Putin of official corruption. This charge of corruption, while true, was a screen for these oligarchs' conflict over control of fossil fuel assets, since Putin wanted the lion's share for his group. Putin's judges threw Khodorkovsky in jail on counter charges, but Khodorkovsky remained trusted by the Russian people and a significant liability to Putin's regime for many years. Khodorkovsky was finally released on appeal by the German Minister of the Interior, Hans-Dietrich Genscher, one of the German leaders most supportive of connections between the two nations, showing how the battle between the two Russian groups impacted European oil flows and engaged the EU oligarchs.

To avoid losing power from his conflict with Khodorkovsky, Putin exploited Russian nationalism to distract and gain support from the masses. Struggles between groups, such as this conflict over oil rights, are so dangerous to oligarchs that they seek to quell them whenever possible, hence Genscher's intervention. In another example of oligarchic conflict, the civil war between Julius Caesar's party, the *Populares*, and the *Optimates* in the Senate destroyed the Roman Republic. Globalist and nationalist oligarchs currently struggle in the US; the outcome is uncertain and bleak.

Next, we cite an example of individuals seeking power and wealth through a corporate network. This group conflicted with another network comprised of state government, private equity, and real estate holdings. Between 2010 and 2012, Aubrey McClendon, the founder of Chesapeake Energy, acquired control of public and private Pennsylvania lands by offering pipeline and fracking deals that initially appeared profitable to landowners. However, McClendon's contracts, contrary to usual practice, forced those landowners to pay both principal and interest on what amounted to a multibillion loan to its pipeline affiliate, Chesapeake Midstream Partners. Both landowners and Pennsylvania state officials, finding that they had been deceived about their future profits, balked at the unfavorable contracts once they realized the cost. The landowners had power in the statehouse, as did some of Chesapeake's stockholders. The State of Pennsylvania officials, landholders, and stockholders formed an alliance to force McClendon out.

Those deals alone did not unseat McClendon. He sealed his fate by personally borrowing money from Chesapeake. The combination of corrupt personal finances and shifting costs from Chesapeake to the landowners undid McClendon. It usually takes such a combination of business and personal problems to dismantle a strong oligarch's network. In fact, the network was not destroyed. Although McClendon was subsequently sued and deposed from office, then died in a mysterious automobile crash, the corporation is returning to profitability even without a magnetic leader.

Next, we point to those assets added to an (e)state by an acquiring oligarch. These assets are either in the same country and language, or they have a different culture. When culture and language are the same, it is easier to maintain them because the current and acquired workers, having similar customs, coexist in order to preserve the old conditions. Corporate examples include the acquisitions of Tivoli by IBM and Flash by Adobe. Although these corporate cultures differed in some respects, many customs were similar. Existing workers and managers worked well together, and personal connections reconciled important cultural differences.

The acquired employees kept in mind that the manager of their former company was no different than the new boss, meaning that managers have similar profit motives. The same class and control mechanisms exist. To avert the brunt of acquired workers' skepticism, the acquiring company, for its part, should not radically alter the acquired company's rules, but make the transition seem transparent when integrating workers with the new parent.

When assets are acquired by a corporation differing in language, customs, or laws, greater difficulties arise. Careful attention to detail is needed to make foreign acquisitions profitable, even in these days of cheap cross-border capital flows. If, for example, local production facilities had not employed US workers, BMW and Toyota would have had difficulty growing US market share. State and corporate resistance was too great. Importantly, if a trusted local manager is on site, problems are seen when they occur and can be quickly remedied, but if no one is on site, difficulties are only recognized when it may be too late.

In this way, Deutsche Bank suffered in managing its US subsidiary in the 1990s. Deutsche Bank had brought in a charismatic German manager, Hermann Seiler, who governed the US subsidiary under the same culture as in the parent company back in Germany. When he hired a US technology leader as chief information officer from one of the local banks, the new CIO was quickly convinced by the current US managers that the German plan and culture were unprofitable, and that the new German software was inferior to existing code. Seiler meanwhile was back at the parent company thinking he had succeeded. The US CIO sided with the US managers, and the German leadership only heard about it when it was too late to do anything. The Germans were forced to fire their new CIO and abandon their plan to run the US subsidiary with the German global systems, allowing the US middle managers to retain self-dealing relationships with software and services vendors in order to maintain their old system.

If a company, in the absence of local leadership, is not manipulated by its middle managers, as Deutsche Bank was, workers are satisfied by prompt access to any senior manager. Wishing to be thought good employees, workers have more cause to love their jobs and to fear losing them. The workers, of course, have their own culture to confirm their common interests. Thus, any company that would attack a market from afar must act cautiously. When a charismatic manager resides locally, market share can only be wrested from the acquiring company with great difficulty.

On the other hand, because corporations are complex, market share can be lost through other methods, such as competitive marketing and design strategies, as when Audi took market share from BMW or as Tesla is now taking mind-share from builders of internal combustion engines, initiating thereby a broad cultural shift. Here we see how bold innovation can change even the basic rules of business.

Corporations can follow another, less expensive, and appropriate initial incursion by sending sales and marketing teams to one or two places in the new territory. These teams support access to markets and help build networks there. Compared to starting a new business or building factories, a company using this method spends little on sales teams or advertising. With less cash, a company can increase profit and offend only a minority of the firms from which it takes market share.

In the case of political organizations, citizens are often offended by a foreigner's presence on their soil, especially during this renaissance of nationalism. Nevertheless, those whom that presence offends, remaining small and scattered, although they complain loudly, are barely able to injure an expanding state. Meanwhile the rest, being uninjured, are easily won over. The weak resistance of the French against German occupation in WWII, Iraqi Sunni resistance to the US in the second Gulf War, and the Chinese resistance to Manchu invasions are good examples. Most people are unwilling to engage in violence. If the state itself cannot resist the aggressor, the people usually cannot rise up and overthrow the invader.

Parallel conditions operate in business networks. Corporate competitors are anxious not to err for fear that your expansion finds a weakness in their sector. Their caution can be exploited by expanding firms or political forces. Aggressive expansion temporarily wins the day.

In the long run, however, you must work to align the cultures of acquired states with yours, as the Chinese are attempting in Tibet. Otherwise, armed resistance will threaten your hegemony as the state may reform around long-term resistance as happened in many of the third-world colonies of European powers. Change occurs by divergence.

Regarding aggression, we must remark that you should either treat people well or crush them because while they can avenge themselves of lighter injuries, serious ones disable them. Therefore, the injury done to a nation or a company in war or market competition ought to be such that you do not fear revenge from competing oligarchs with substantial assets. US policy toward North Korea and its military oligarchy might follow this precept except for a contemporary anomaly linked to nuclear weapons and the potential destruction of Seoul.

The experiences of the Soviet Union in Afghanistan and the US in the Middle East are excellent examples. By maintaining armed men in those areas, instead of developing profitable client states, like Israel or Cuba, both nations invested huge sums with minimal returns. Their garrisons consumed so many resources that their acquisitions became losses. Many more leaders were exasperated because the whole state was injured. The expenses of the Soviet occupation of Afghanistan might even be associated with state bankruptcy and the fall of the Soviet empire.

By shifting the garrison around, as the US did in Iraq, both citizens and soldiers suffered and became hostile. Many Iraqi citizens became enemies of the US. Beaten on their own ground, they were still able to improvise explosive devises and engage suicide bombers. Many reorganized with the Islamic State. This could have been avoided had not the oil oligarchs associated with George W. Bush's administration forced their military garrison on Iraq.

For multiple reasons then, military bases are as useless to a nation as colonies are useful, except strategically as passive presences, largely unused against native populations who should ultimately be coerced to pay for them as Trump hopes the Europeans will. Arms manufacturers on the other hand benefit from such garrisons and may be understood, along with the oil companies, as the interests driving such ill-considered expenses. With each armed foray into Iraq, the US increased its expenses and reduced its state profits. US President George H. W. Bush wisely withdrew his armies before they needed to occupy Iraq. He saved money while gaining the support of the Kuwaiti and other Arab leaders as their protector. In contrast, George W. Bush incurred approximately a trillion dollars of losses to the state and the enmity of Arab nations with his invasion of Iraq in 2002 while Vice President Dick Cheney's corporate allies profited more than fifty billion dollars. Such imbalance benefits only the few and can be understood as business networks using government assets for profit.

These armed efforts not only cost good cash and good will, but destabilized the region. In neighboring Syria, citizens, stirred up by the chaos generated by Western interests, rose up against President Bashar al-Assad. Even the peace-loving US President Barack Obama was forced to deal with Islamic State forces, first with an intelligent air-power-only attack. But now the US has been dragged into the mire of regional politics, along with Russia, Iran, Britain, France, and Turkey. Such a conflict of multiple cultures looks as chaotic as the Crusades where European, Mongol, Egyptian, and multiple Arab oligarchs collided. Syria has become the perfect foreign policy focus for a muddled Trump administration. The press cannot fit such a multilateral conflict into its binary model, pointing first to one bilateral conflict and then another as the situation cycles out of control. The media focus the people's moral indignation first on one situation and then another while Trump's ruling oligarchs, operating in the shadows, accumulate assets at home.

This wider war temporarily supports the oil oligarchies such as those based in Saudi Arabia and the Emirates, but destroys infrastructure in the region without establishing good relations. Emigration from collapsing Middle Eastern societies then provokes US and European nationalism, strengthening global religious conflict and helping set the stage for a formidable Islamic bloc while Western nations retrench. In any case, such uncertainty is not helpful to local oligarchs who are less able to support their networks and pacify their people. Only those oligarchs in control of state regimes, such as Trump's cabinet and their associated corporations, can truly benefit themselves and their networks by selling arms, although capital markets also help in a broad way across multiple industries.

To better defend a client state, an oligarchy must weaken the most powerful among the client state's neighbors. Thus, the US attacked the wrong nation when it invaded Iraq. The US failed to take care that no equal foreign power like Russia, by any accident, gained a foothold in the Middle East as it allowed China to do in South America, where US gunboat diplomacy has been disliked by local oligarchs for generations, or in Africa, where populations are growing. It appears that Russia will now attempt to reunite Syria under Assad, although situational complexity precludes effective prediction.

Through its inaction, the US forced Russia to protect its Syrian military bases, and thereby introduced a powerful competitor. Initially Russian involvement in Syria distracted it from the Ukraine, but the Trump administration's support for Russia reopens negotiations about Russia's former client state. Such chaotic interactions emanated from Cheney's initial decision to line the pockets of the oil patch oligarchs.

On the other hand, when it seeks stable markets through soft power, the US uses appropriate methods. It sends salesmen and political operatives into countries and promotes the wonders of US products. It buys and maintains friendly relations with the local oligarchs against their competitors. It suppresses nationalistic powers as when local businessmen in many nations support incursions against multinational corporate competition. It does not allow strong foreign powers to gain sway, although a tremendous military force is strategically deployed to keep those adjacent powers at bay. Unsurprisingly, this military deployment bolsters participating oligarchs' coffers. The conflict between military and soft-power oligarchs remains a key policy problem for the US government.

Europe after WWII is a good example of the value of soft power. Despite the wreckage of war, the US stayed friendly with both France and Germany, contained the Soviet Union, and drove Fascists out of some enclaves while installing anti-Communists where it suited US containment strategies, while rebuilding corporate assets and connections through the Marshall Plan. Yet the German and French oligarchs until recently didn't secure permission to increase their military power. Now resurgent nationalism throughout the developed world drives greater military spending and risks pan-European conflict. Globalists, nationalist conservatives, and realist oligarchs are locked in unpredictable negotiation for control of many governments and budgetary foci.

A judicious oligarch addresses not only present troubles, but also prepares energetically for possible future scenarios. When an industrial illness like climate change is foreseen, it is easy to remedy. But if, for short-term gains, the oligarchy waits until the forests are already compromised and the oceans acidified, and it remains unwilling to face the actual nature of the problem, available remedies may be too late to avoid disrupting civil order. The rise of ruling oligarchs with their delusional metaphors in major nations such as the US or Russia is another way to avoid dealing with the disruptions of climate change. The collapse of current oligarchic states and social arrangements will precede crop failures due to climate change. Are developed countries focusing their finances effectively?

A risk-aware actuarial approach would initiate broad plans early. For example, your children are not likely not die while playing in the streets, but providing a playground for their safety is a prudent outlay. Spending money prophylactically against climate change provides a platform for solutions and enables adoption of lower risk solutions. While this spending is initially inconvenient to leadership and the people alike, the impact of climate change is blunted. Instead, oligarchs with few exceptions appear to be taking an all-or-nothing approach based on binary beliefs rather than judicious risk management. In this way, oligarchy, although as common in nature as in human politics, seems oddly ill-suited to administering changes in how resources are used for energy, transportation, agriculture, and construction. Conflicts arise throughout the system that reduce the ability of the network to defend itself. Nationalism disrupts important strategies.

Operating with the correct assumption that the future cannot be accurately predicted, climate change deniers ignore that one can readily project the problems that will occur if earth's climate becomes less supportive of humanity's current systems. If this possibility were zero, then deniers would be correct, but as the probability of climate disruption increases, so energy, transportation, and agricultural policies must adjust.

By fighting against Russia, US liberals ignore how, in the long run, peace is needed with the Russians who control the largest northern reaches of the planet. Without Siberia available to the peoples of the earth, climate change is even more likely to pit every oligarch's network against every other one and the planet against all. Without strong alliances with Russia and Canada, the species will too soon, even with such a large and widely distributed population, find continuity difficult. Nevertheless, pacifying the people with climate change denial allows an oligarch to work in the background to build safe havens in enough appropriate regions to secure some of them against climate devastation of hard assets.

CHAPTER IV: WHY THE RELIGIOUS OLIGARCHS OF IRAN, SUBJUGATED BY THE US, REBELLED AGAINST REZA SHAH PAHLAVI, FORCING HIS ABDICATION, AND WHY SUCH WAS NOT THE CASE IN UKRAINE

Holding a newly acquired state is difficult. Existing leadership may thwart challenges to a nascent state in one of two ways. First, a strong leader, who subordinates others through the form of autocracy, allows existing oligarchs to hold onto their assets and companies as long as they support the regime and assist in governing the state. A state thus governed should fear tyranny only when its leader controls both security apparatus and the courts. Therefore, other oligarchs must guard these institutions carefully through separation of powers.

In a major corporation, a strong leader controls business relationships, production, patents, finances, and retains the loyalty of key employees. He needs subordinate oligarchs because he cannot successfully manage either the country or company without their expertise, backing, and connections. If he eliminates them, fearing that they will rise against him, he will not maintain control for long. The despotisms that occasionally ruled the Roman Republic showed the instability of a state that tried to eliminate the power and control of its oligarchs and disrupt the connections of their networks. States with strong leaders persist only when that leader builds sustainable institutions that can manage the state for the long term. Few such leaders have actually ruled, although history is fond of building narratives about them.

In the second way, a figurehead or elected leader governs with support from existing oligarchs, a political party, and other citizens and employees. Once this second method of governance takes control, building assets and political connections, oligarchs remain strong as long as they continue to maintain the impression that they govern with concurrence of the people. This kind of state or company can last for centuries as long as external forces such as foreign armies, disruptive technology, or climate change do not intervene.

Examples of the first method of governance in our time are prerevolutionary Iran, Singapore, and Russia under Putin. The second method is broadly represented by post-Soviet Ukraine, China, and the democracies of the US and EU. The Roman Republic also appeared to follow this method, except that the wealthy members of the oligarchy ruled as the managers and magistrates of the state. The US is moving in that last direction with the election of Trump, a wealthy oligarch who is also now head of state. Trump fills his cabinet with other wealthy individuals like Wilbur Ross, Rex Tillerson, Betsy DeVos, and Steven Mnuchin. Other important posts are filled by oligarchs associated with the Koch brothers. Trump and his conservative allies may attempt to move toward an autocratic form of governance, but civil institutions, courts, and the security state are not yet under his control and will temporarily push back even if he receives support or concurrence from the majority of oligarchs. Significant divergence is developing among oligarchs in many states that has in the past led to war.

Iran, for example, elected a popular Prime Minister, Mohammad Mosaddegh, in 1951. His National Front government was composed of labor, intellectuals, an Islamic party, and liberals influenced by Western democracies. After Mosaddegh's election, the National Front attempted to tax and otherwise limit oil company activities. When British Petroleum refused to negotiate, the National Front nationalized the oil business. The global oil companies complained to US President Dwight Eisenhower who, in 1953, authorized the CIA to overthrow the National Front's government. The US then installed Reza Pahlavi as Shah to support the oil companies. Those who insist that the state operates in another realm separate from corporations might consider these events, as well as examples of the actions of US corporations in South and Central America.

Once in power, Pahlavi divided his nation into provinces based on its nineteenth-century monarchist structure. He sent ministers to each province, propagating power through these traditional channels. Pahlavi's ministers were only his administrators. He did not share his power with other leaders, thereby weakening the state. He did not seek support of the workers' alliances such as the Toiler's Party or the crafts and guilds that Mosaddegh used as his base of power. This rising class opposed the Shah throughout his reign. He shifted and changed administrators as he chose without respect to the inherent leaders in the provinces. These changes and his failure to align with national groups other than affiliates of the oil cartel weakened his regime. Oil and other business sectors often seek greater

CHAPTER IV: WHY THE RELIGIOUS OLIGARCHS OF IRAN, SUBJUGATED BY... 19

freedom to operate by weakening state controls. Finally, even the power of the US was insufficient to control the people, a plurality of whom must consent for an oligarch to succeed.

Pahlavi, through the press, began to attack the rising power of the Shia clerics. Led by Ayatollah Khomeini, who lived in exile, these clerics organized local mullahs and through them the people, since the lower classes in Iran were strongly affiliated with Islam. Thus, by building a network that included the mullahs, the working classes, and the intelligentsia, the clerics, who had been waiting in the wings, were able to take over. These ecclesiastical oligarchs then quickly suppressed the democratic leaders who desperately attempted to ally themselves with them.

Thus, three leading groups—the liberals, the Shah with foreign support, and the religious leaders—vied for power. The liberals' failure to align with another oligarchic channel or foreign support disrupted their connection to the government. The Shah's antiquated regional connections allowed the Shia clerics to build a controlling domestic network, although initially with difficulty. They have held power since 1979 and have built a formidable state that projects power throughout the region.

Engaging an indigenous group of interests within a parliamentary form of governance, the leaders of the Ukraine, who took over after the Russian-backed President Victor Yanukovych was deposed, were placed in the midst of a body of elected officials, and were then acknowledged and supported by their constituents and EU leaders. President Petro Poroshenko, Prime Minister Volodymyr Groysman, and other ruling oligarchs are required by article 83 of the Ukrainian Constitution to form a governing coalition by factions that represent a majority of the parliament. Thus, Constitutional power in Ukraine is determined and directed by homogeneous groups that dominate government in its form.

Component groups thereby maintain their own prerogatives though a Federalist system. The prime minister takes these powers away at his peril. Thus, when the Kiev government attempted to cut ties between the Eastern provinces and Russia, both the industrialists of eastern Ukraine and many of the people in the east, who speak Russian, resisted. While no one can predict whether Russia, unopposed in its core sphere of influence, will use military force to depose this well constituted government with European affiliations, Ukraine is stably structured with oligarchic intent. With European funding and the support of major corporations, the Ukraine can survive even the loss of its eastern provinces. But the Shah's government was always dependent on foreign power and puppet administrators rather than on the more solid basis of collaboration with the indigenous leaders of Iran. Such governments are always unlikely to last. The same is likely true if an individual, like McClendon, is too central to the operations of a major corporation.

Considering their situation, the ayatollahs had difficulty seizing the provinces of Iran from the Shah's monarchic structure because the secular and religious networks were disconnected and at odds with each other. Religious leaders could expect little advantage from an alliance with the Shah's ministers, who were corrupt and did not have the support of the people. Hence, when the Islamic party attacked the Shah's party, it found his oligarchs united against them and difficult to unseat. For their part, the ayatollahs had to rely more on their own strength and the support of the masses, rather than on a revolt of the Shah's minions.

Nevertheless, once the Shah had been forced out of office, the Islamic party had nothing to fear but the Western powers. However, since those powers had no adherents left in Iran, no credit with the people, and no regional oligarchs to support their interests, the Westerners quickly lost control. Since the conquering Islamic party did not rely on Western powers before its victory, it did not need them afterward. Within a few months after Shah Pahlavi was deposed, the Muslim Student Followers of the Imam's Line, loyal to the ayatollahs, took fifty-two US embassy officials hostage. Displeasure with the Shah's corrupt government and foreign intervention made it easy for the ayatollahs, students, and security forces to hold the country through its federal system rather than through a big man. Even the Supreme Leader of Iran acts as a judge and arbiter rather than dictator, owing his power to the security apparatus, administrative government, and the people's piety.

It will take a great effort to unseat the ayatollahs unless an alliance of Western powers can separate them from the secular leaders of the provinces of Iran and empower the latter. These key regional leaders supply food and other necessities, while the mullahs have the ear of the people. Also, if through any insupportable cruelty, the ayatollahs lose the allegiance of the indigenous leaders of the provinces and of the people, their power may wane. But the ayatollahs, unlike the leaders of Islamic State, do not engage visibly in corrupt practices, such as beheading and raping civilians, although they have been accused of widespread administrative corruption. Because of their balanced approach to power, they are taken seriously by Western and Asian leaders. Western cultural resentment against Iran and Israel's battles with Iran over religion endanger peaceful relations. These difficulties do not stem from the weakness of the Iranian government, but rather from a larger battle over sphere of influence.

Back in the Ukraine, in a manner parallel to the Iranian situation, Putin, angered by losing so valuable and traditional a client state to Western Ukrainians, easily gained support of industrialists in Eastern Ukraine who opened the way for pro-Russian forces to the Eastern provinces. But to hold Ukraine afterwards, Putin would meet with infinite difficulties, created both by those who assisted him and by those he crushed, because he would be fragmenting an historic Ukrainian state. Destructive oligarchic conflict between the interests of the Eastern industrialists with ties to Russia and the Western provinces with their ties to Europe, between industrial and agricultural leaders, benefits only those seeking to weaken the state. The focus of the Western press on the character of Putin misses the core conflict of oligarchic interests within Ukraine that drives the war.

For Putin, military action is problematic, since it is insufficient to exterminate the army of Kiev's central government. Leaders remain in Western Ukraine with alliances to Europe, and Europe, being in need of Ukrainian grain, will make Western Ukrainian oligarchs the heads of fresh movements against the East. Since the East can neither satisfy nor exterminate them, the Western oligarchs can wreak havoc whenever the opportunity arises. Such unpredictability is rarely in the interests of a local oligarch. Putin will always have to consider the independent spirit of the Ukrainians, including his adversaries in the agricultural West and even his adherents in the industrial East. This is why Russia seeks a federal state and destabilization of the Ukrainian government rather than annexation to Russia, at least for now.

No matter how well constituted the current government in Kiev may be, Ukraine is in Russia's sphere of influence and will always have difficulties if it does not find some common ground with Russian oligarchs. Because of this combined history and geography, Europe will not resist Putin's military in Ukraine should he decide on that course of action, although he doesn't want more sanctions placed on his government and leading oligarchs. Russia, on the other hand, because of US recent military inaction, justified by war fatigue, has had to turn to defending its port in Syria. But one can be sure that Putin's oligarchs are maneuvering behind the scenes to try to gain control of trade and industry in Eastern Ukraine and in Crimea. Putin's power depends on those oligarchs' support, but with the recent election of Trump, he may find less conflict with the US.

In this chapter, we showed how the form of government is only partly responsible for the channels through which it operates. Even when the form is linked tightly to operations, such as in the purer democracy described by Herodotus or the tightly held autocracy, leading citizens still contend for power and access to key assets. Oligarchic democracy, oligarchic autocracy—form follows function.

In all these cases, the success of any regime depends on the support of leading citizens. When these oligarchs collide, as is occurring in the US, due to the failure of globalization to address the needs of white middle- and working-class voters who are supported by libertarian oligarchs, conflicts of interest must be resolved through networks of influence and serious trading of assets, or grave battles will commence. Neither the formal channels of government nor those of the market alone can maintain social stability under these conditions. Nationalists, realists, and liberal globalists can all understand this situation.

Nevertheless, these different groups seem to have difficulty negotiating. Their difficulties have perhaps emerged because they have accumulated groups of followers based on false premises. They have used the emotional biases of received culture to convince these followers to act against their own self-interest. Such situations will always make the oligarchs' actions and those of their followers appear irrational when viewed from the outside.

Network connections, both cultural and regional, are the keys to successful control of wealth-producing assets and governance at all levels. Groups that might have negotiated solutions to their differences in a society where leadership encourages unity and offers hope, rather than promulgating fear and factionalism, become less able to communicate as they fight increasingly closely contested elections where the issues are increasingly removed from control of assets or promoting the well-being of the people. Methods of gaining adherents through strident media pronouncements, emotional appeals, and efficient voter suppression become more likely to cause irrevocable divergence and cultural differences that even centuries cannot heal.

2: On the Details of Acquisition and Management of Organizations

CHAPTER V: CONCERNING THE WAY TO GOVERN FIRMS AND STATES THAT ARE ACCUSTOMED TO OPERATE UNDER THEIR OWN (BY-)LAWS

If companies and nations have been accustomed to working under their own rules, there are three paths for those who wish to acquire them. The first is to ruin them. The next is for a new leader to establish a headquarters there. The third is to permit them to continue to work under their own (by-)laws, while the new oligarch skims the profit, checks their financials regularly, and manages to keep them friendly by paying close attention to their organization's culture. Because both state and corporate governance are styled by their leaders, people at all levels know that they cannot do their jobs without the leaders' support. They do their utmost to support the regime, especially if they have a government pension and corporate stock plan. Acquirers will manage a state and company accustomed to independence most easily by means of its own people and culture. Attempting to rule against the grain of the existing organizational culture has resulted in the downfall of many regimes.

Examples vary widely, but have similar characteristics. Leadership cannot have a presence in every province and subsidiary. Foreign uniforms in city squares and transportation hubs make people turn their heads away. The empty office of an absent executive reinforces whatever bad feeling exists against the parent company. Proxy governments often turn against the colonizing state. Difficulties arise if the managers left in place revert to the alliances and practices they used prior to the takeover as already mentioned in the case of Deutsche Bank. And sometimes the success of an acquired company was due to its unique style and processes.

In its takeover bid of AstraZeneca in 2014, Pfizer didn't address the concern that valuable research projects would be shelved, therefore weakening the pipeline if the company was carved up to fit Pfizer's US operating model. So, AstraZeneca's CEO Pascal Soriot did what all defending leaders must do and painted for his employees a happy picture of life as an independent company. He argued that AstraZeneca's investors had not appreciated the possible wonders in the company's pipeline, especially the cancer portfolio. Using this tactic, Soriot avoided the takeover.

Pfizer's approach, throughout its pursuit of AstraZeneca, was driven by the benefits to its shareholders, cost savings, and tax minimization. But Pfizer's CEO Ian Read's approach was too aggressive from the outset, as it ignored AstraZeneca's independent identity. Pfizer again tried to reduce its tax burden by taking over Allergan and failed again. Read ignored that any company should support the jurisdictions in which it profits rather than always trying to game the system. Apparently, too, Read's top-heavy management style struggles to prosper on its own. He seeks to compete at every level instead of recognizing how important alliances, connections, and mutual benefit are to success. Leaders of all types of organizations can learn from Read's failures.

Both the Chinese administration of Tibet and Israeli forces in Palestine might also benefit from this perspective, as they have taken over from or are still in conflict with indigenous oligarchs and existing cultures. China might with little effort include some of the Tibetan traditional oligarchs and their people in the benefits of development projects. The current Chinese effort to disperse the Tibetan people will only solidify their allegiance to their traditional culture as diaspora did for the Jews, African-American populations, and Gypsies among others. The Chinese destruction of traditional Tibetan culture cannot be justified by citing a litany of atrocities performed by the ruling oligarchy of lamas and aristocrats. The Chinese approach itself is quite brutal and disenfranchises Tibetan asset holders, who are local oligarchs with long memories and financial connections to political and artistic communities in the US and EU.

Israel's conflict with Palestine remains equally inappropriate, although it is easy to understand how it began. So much writing about the Israeli and Palestinian conflict has been published from both sides that we hesitate to remark even faintly that the solution is manifest and has been often cited.

CHAPTER V: CONCERNING THE WAY TO GOVERN FIRMS AND STATES THAT... 25

Oligarchs and interest groups on both sides, however, remain unwilling to relinquish any part of their holdings, so the transparent solution remains overshadowed by cultural differences, land grabs, and traditional resentments that arise from regimes that are accustomed to operate under their own laws.

When companies, on the other hand, are accustomed to obeying a domineering single oligarch, employees cannot easily govern themselves. For this reason, John Thain, when put in power by leading shareholders and government administrators, easily continued Merrill Lynch's militaristic management style from former CEO Stan O'Neal. Bank of America CEO Kenneth Lewis then acquired Merrill with Thain at the helm during the 2007 financial crisis. Lewis thereby gained Merrill for his coterie and secured it quite easily, even as he complained that he was pressured by the US Treasury to acquire bankrupt Merrill and its debts.

The fact was that Merrill became an easy target when it got in trouble because its management team was too dependent on O'Neal's command-control structure. Relying on a strong individual, whether it be a corporate manager or a political leader like Trump, does not endure as well as relying on the network of management and workers who mutually benefit from corporate and government policies. It must also be pointed out group decisions are slower and execution more labored than those under an empowered individual leader, but that leader must be authorized by the group for decisions to lead to sustainable results.

In truly independent countries and companies, there is more vitality, greater hatred of the takeover, and more desire for vengeance after the takeover. Such countries and companies will never allow the memory of their former liberty to be forgotten, as we see with Tibet and Texas. The safest corporate takeover strategy then is to destroy organizational entities with independent cultures, such as AOL and other tech companies, such as TheGlobe.com and WorldCom, that eluded takeovers during the dotcom bubble. If the acquiring oligarch has a high percentage of stock ownership in the company, then resistance is likely to be less, while the size of the CEO's golden parachute, despite its bad press, has been shown to have little or no effect on the likelihood of takeovers.

The same problems occur when a state is taken over. If the acquired country or region was accustomed to independent rule, and power was shared among various interest groups, it will be more difficult to control unless you can make the people think that you will rule with a light hand and allow them to maintain their cultural biases. Trump and his libertarian funders will have difficulty controlling the US without collaborating with Democrats and leaders of multinational corporations. Eastern Ukraine supports Putin because he appears to represent its traditional culture, language, and business. Strategic immigration of Russians to Eastern Ukraine also acts as a pretext for takeover. Syrian refugees fleeing civil war is not an example of strategic immigration, but rather a result of a regime terrorizing its people and refusing to address climate change in its eastern farming regions.

Taking over a state dominated by a narrowly based oligarchy is easier if the state was autocratic as in Tibet and Palestine. But replacing their cultures is quite another and more difficult matter. The US found no resistance, for example, when it took over Iraq from Saddam Hussein's faction based on his extended clan around Tikrit, but the successor state failed to live up to its promise of equality under the law. It alienated the Sunnis who, being used to governing not only themselves but also the Shia of Iraq, returned to their older alliances under threat from Shia affiliations with Iran and the Shia government's failure to include Sunni leaders in the process of governance.

Chapter VI: Concerning New Oligarchies Acquired by Skill

Do not be surprised if, in speaking of new firms, we cite the most effective examples of oligarchic strategy and operational skill. Of course, not every leader is a great innovator. People usually walk on paths broken by others. A wise oligarch follows the tracks of eminent people and learns from those supreme in their fields. Even if your ability does not equal that of your predecessor's, at least it will resemble it, and that is often sufficient. Those similarities, as with this book, may improve understanding. Further, imitators are unable to precisely copy innovators, and, since evolution occurs through divergence, using a great deed as a model changes outcomes. In any case, you can act like the marksman who, planning to hit a distant target and knowing the limits of your available leverage, takes aim above the bullseye to hit the mark.

In an entirely new venture, the operational ability of the team that creates it determines whether it achieves profitability. Often a brilliant creative team is not able to run the firm profitably. If that is the case, venture capitalists replace the originating group with more professional management, allowing the original team to create new enterprises. Remember how many generals Abraham Lincoln fired before finding William T. Sherman and Ulysses S. Grant. Remember how many failures the Koch brothers shepherded through their conservative campaigns until they found the right balance of strategic alliance and direct operational control.

Rising to the oligarchy presupposes either ability or good fortune. Those who relied least on fortune established the strongest firms. It facilitates matters when entrepreneurs have no other business. Then they are compelled to manage the new firm in person, improving their chances of success. Trump will have endless difficulties as president negotiating between the interests of his own companies and the interests of the nation. Twitter CEO Jack Dorsey must also manage Square. Managing Tesla and the Gigafactory, Solar City, and SpaceX requires many different skills with the additional risks of integration common to all conglomerates.

Among those who, by their own ability and not through fortune alone, have risen to be leading oligarchs, we suggest that Moses, Ross Perot, Jennifer Holmgren, Steve Jobs, and Michael Bloomberg are excellent examples. Although Moses seems a problematic icon, since he was merely executing the will of God, he ought to be admired, if only for that configuration of self and situation which made him worthy to speak with a deity.

Those who founded great companies should not be considered inferior to Moses, although he had such a prodigious patron. Perhaps the continuing sponsorship of the eternal individual helps an organization to last while mere mortals rarely bequeath firms or states that endure as long as religions do. For that reason, many states have encouraged their leaders to assume the mantle of gods. One wonders what methods, such as films and holidays, corporate oligarchs will use in the future to enshrine their founders and encourage loyalty through the aegis of a mythic leader who mimics the self-image of many aspiring individuals. Pharaohs, Japanese and Chinese emperors, Natchez rulers, Roman emperors, and others ruled their states as deities.

It is important to note how the religion of St. Paul, that timeless oligarch, federated independent synagogues to fund a common church. That operational process also modeled the Holy Trinity by Athanasius and later St. Basil who proposed a single deity of three parts. This structure of the deity posed that frequent conflicts among the three parts could only be adjudicated through bureaucratic church institutions that attempted to avoid and thus slow change. How often a CEO encounters conflicts between different parts of a corporation. To achieve success in sales may impact funds allocated to research and development. Actions required to maintain power, to achieve moral virtue in the public arena, and to further the stated character of the organization may conflict. These diverse goals cannot be accomplished from any one point of view. Oligarchic power needs managers at many levels with latitude to act on their own behalf, so long as they do not compromise the whole.

Contrary to the image that many ambitious individuals have of themselves, a single person rarely manages alone. To create a powerful organization and especially a cultural force, teams of people together support the most significant changes. The actions and lives of innovators show that they also owe much to their surroundings and to receptive conditions. Strong, well-heeled supporters; opportunities such as inventions; failures of prior leaders; and receptive market climates bring innovators material to mold into new ventures. These organizations and cultural changes operate more like ecosystems than through prime movers, genius individuals, or essences. Hence, maintaining balance in your organism, your organization, and the biosphere remains the crucial skill of leadership. When your own balance teeters, which happens to all individuals, your organization must be operated by skilled subordinates and a stable form of governance.

Without those opportunities created by favorable conditions, the powers of innovators might have been wasted, and without those powers the opportunity would have come in vain. Among those pre-conditions of accomplishment are the societies where innovators live. It is easy in the US for a company to succeed, since the society has built and maintained smooth roads, sturdy power grids, and other infrastructure. The tax structure also supports new ventures. A new business in the US does not have to bribe too many officials in order to begin. However much the entrepreneur pats him or herself on the back at joining the oligarchy, a new oligarch must recognize and reward the society that supported his or her rise to power, since it is like the earth to the farmer: no matter how hard the farmer works, if the soil is not fertile, the crops will not flourish.

If oligarchs fail to support society and only pursue their own short-term interests, they will seem rich and powerful, but their power will be hollow, and the people will not support them. We see such differences in the long-term success of oligarchies supported by the geography of Venice, the Magna Carta alliance, and the meritocracy of the Chinese bureaucracy, as opposed to the short-lived states of the self-serving. Even those short-lived states depended on strong supporting teams. Josef Stalin depended on Molotov, Voroshilov, Beria, and Malenkov, and Adolf Hitler depended on Himmler, Goring, Goebbels, Bormann, von Ribbentrop, Speer, and others. Let the leader who thinks only of himself think again.

So much depends on initial conditions, and these conditions change continuously, requiring recalculation. It was necessary for Moses to find the people of Israel enslaved and oppressed by the Egyptians, so they were disposed to follow him. It was necessary that Perot's ideas were ignored by IBM brass, so that he could become the founder of Electronic Data Systems. It was necessary that Bloomberg should find traders discontented with scattered real-time information delivery systems, and that Dow Jones should be soft and weak from lack of competition. Holmgren might not have shown her ability had she not found climate change such a potential inhibitor to regulated business. Jobs could not have founded Apple without Steve Wozniak, new technologies to assemble, and a receptive alternative culture in California. These conditions were indispensable to their success.

Thus, helping the people and the society as a whole to prosper with you extends those auspicious conditions supporting progress. Infrastructure is another environmental factor that not only helps the people prosper, but facilitates transportation, communication, and an awareness of the value of the oligarchy that builds and manages those structures. If the roads are full of potholes, the bridges appear risky to cross, and water and electric services are intermittent, the people spend more time worrying about how to get to work than actually working. Good infrastructure facilitates building new companies and investing in new ideas. The willingness of government leaders and bond holders to invest in modern infrastructure makes a nation proud and pleased to support the oligarchs who provide those facilities.

The difficulties in creating a new company also arise from the untested rules and methods that you introduce to establish your invention and build its market. There is nothing more difficult to control, more perilous to conduct, or more uncertain of success than introducing a new order of things. The innovator has as enemies all those who have prospered under the old conditions and tepid defenders among those who may do well under the new, since they are as yet uncertain of the advantage of the new thing. Their coolness arises also from fear of their opponents, who have the law and habit on their side, and from the incredulity of people, who do not readily believe in new things until they experience them.

Resistance to solar and wind power and electric transportation arises as much from overcoming existing culture as higher cost. Most people have an aversion to change and resistance to solutions. Changing how work is done requires energy to learn new skills and risks failure. People, along with all other living organisms, seek to survive with as little expenditure of energy as possible. Whenever those who are hostile to change have the opportunity to attack the change agents, they do it like partisans, while futurists defend without foundations, endangering the innovator. The same is true with new strategies in culture that encounter the same resistances to change and inhibitors to success. Until an environmental culture clearly supports the interests of both leadership and the people, until leading oligarchs are visibly threatened by climate change, the resistance of climate change deniers to renewables will remain strong and find strong adherents.

If we want to discuss this matter thoroughly, we must determine how energy innovators—solar, wind, and electric transport—might build both a smart grid and a supporting culture by themselves or whether they need alliances. Alone, they will succeed with difficulty unless their employees and the voters are already of like mind, which is questionable in any new enterprise and culture. On the other hand, when workers can rely on a network that supports their efforts and aids them in developing sustainable lines of communication, it is easier to build a business and establish a new way of thinking. Building a smart grid and the culture of networks for owners, management, and workers facilitates change at all levels.

Changing the culture of human expansion from one that often ignores the collateral damage of development projects has as prerequisite the effectiveness, stickiness, and sustainability of new technologies. Acceptance of technology that has a lower impact on the environment requires people to change their minds and to alter the way in which they view themselves and their neighbors. Since the end of WWII-fueled economic and technological expansion in the early 1970s, global oligarchs have promoted a culture of selfishness with a false understanding of Darwin's notion of fitness, asserting the primacy of individual desire, and promoting development at all costs. Increasing awareness of the importance of mutual aid, using the theory of mind to understand the needs and suffering of others, and recognizing the real costs of degrading our environment are also prerequisite for an environmental culture to impact individual and group dynamics.

Looking at power, then, from this environmental perspective, it is quite true that armed prophets from Moses to Mohammed have conquered, but they did so with their brethren. The unarmed, solitary ones from Fra Girolamo Savonarola to Jim Bakker have been destroyed. The character of individuals is both unique and similar. While it is easy to persuade people, it is difficult to keep them persuaded. Thus, you must take measures so that, when the shine is off the invention, and the workers and customers no longer feel that the enterprise is special, you may make them believe in the creation by marketing and public relations as if the invention was new and their skills highly prized. Marketing and public relations have made starting new enterprises easier, because they pave the way for new ideas and overcome some of the resistance described above. Their value in promoting new ideas and organizations can be added to the value of oligarchy in maintaining the order and prosperity of the firm and the state. Even an existing form of governance, like democracy, was reinvigorated as a polity of personal desire by the genius of marketing, even as its franchise is eroded by the market's corrupting influence. The same processes can be applied to a society were people's similarity is in their uniqueness, and collective action drives the value of communities and intermediate institutions beyond the state and the corporation.

Oligarchs promoting this environmental culture will be successful beyond starting their companies if they seek advancement within their sphere of influence and do not wander too far from their natural habitat. Perot handled his bid for president badly and should never have run, while Bloomberg, staying within his Wall Street domain, governed for two successful terms and even suborned the New York City electoral process by running for a third term as mayor. And Moses, of course, was successful as long as he remained with the Jews. But because he took too many prerogatives and carried too much Egyptian cultural baggage, he was not able to access the Promised Land. A high level of awareness of your surroundings, your people, and the effects of your actions on your own psyche are some of the components of environmental culture that increase your chances of success in any endeavor. Multilevel awareness of your surroundings is especially effective in implementing a new technology that sustains your ability to profit from environmental resources.

CHAPTER VII: CONCERNING NEW OLIGARCHIES ACQUIRED EITHER BY THE ARMS OF OTHERS OR BY GOOD FORTUNE

Those who by good fortune, unique circumstances, and inheritance become oligarchs have little difficulty in rising to power, but have trouble maintaining effective regimes. There remains a long-term advantage for people who have risen to power by virtue of their skills.

Gifts of power were bestowed on many in Europe by Stalin and Hitler, as well as oligarchs made by London's big bang and Putin's ascension.

Presidents and prime ministers sometimes employ their relatives in positions of power like Trump's appointments of his son-in-law, Jared Kushner, and his daughter, Ivanka, to his government. Sometimes, and this is true for many nations, the top leaders create family cadres that funnel legal and illegal money through personal relationships. We see these situations exposed in China by Xi Jinping's anti-corruption campaign against entrenched cadres who benefited from foreign investment. Ironically for Xi, Trump, even before taking office, leveraged a profitable deal with China worth $400 million for Kushner. After his election, Trump himself received a 10-year exclusive trademark on the use of his name in real-estate development. The same type of patronage, usually hidden behind many shadow corporations, is prevalent in any oligarchic network. You may well wonder whether Trump's bravado in making his patronage transparent helps him retain power or is building toward a collapse of his government.

While these fortunate few benefit from the goodwill and skill of those who elevate them, they don't often have the knowledge required to maintain the position, unless they are coincidentally individuals of great ability, like J.P. Morgan, who was mentored in the secret operations of investment banking by his father. More commonly their lack of skill results in arbitrary and brutal leadership because they feel threatened by the conflicts that their inexperience exposes and are also protective of their inheritance. The use of inherited wealth to undermine the well-being of the people by the Koch brothers, the Bradley Foundation, the Olin/Simon partnership, the Coors heirs, and Richard Mellon Scaife in recent decades proves that protecting wealth endangers society. Every nation sports such examples of lucky inheritors who don't understand the skills through which power is sustained.

Finally, it is unreasonable to expect that the scions of wealth should know how to balance their assets, alliances, and relations with the society that enriched them. These heirs, having never solved difficult problems or directly experienced failure and privation, are often too self-absorbed to unravel the skeins of complex transactions. Hence, merit elevates people to leadership in most countries even though they then benefit their cohorts. Yet a new generation of inherited wealth threatens to weaken developed countries from within as hundreds of fortunes are inherited as the strength of the post-WWII generation fades. The ruins of inherited rulers' failed regimes smolders across humanity's entire history, although building an effective oligarchy directly beneath leadership often proves sustainable.

More often inherited wealth fails to thrive. Doris Duke and her grandnephew, Walker Inman, ran through one of America's great fortunes. The

CHAPTER VII: CONCERNING NEW OLIGARCHIES ACQUIRED EITHER BY THE... 33

Duke Foundation still exists; however, these inheritors ignored their obligations to their society. They also neglected and abused Inman's children, weakening their position, because of public outrage. Only their bankers made money. We cannot build a society on inherited wealth that empowers only the children of hedge-fund managers, fast-food franchisers, and technology leaders.

Some corporations, like many of the dot-com startups, rise unexpectedly. Like most organisms that are born and grow rapidly, they lack time to sink firm roots. Their relations and networks with other corporations spread in such a way that the first storm topples them. Unless those who unexpectedly become corporate leaders develop powerful abilities, they often make grave management mistakes. The ability to find reasonable biological metaphors for human interactions around generational wealth can hardly be coincidental. Individual behavior and human culture share many features of animal and plant interactions. As mentioned, complex systems exhibit similar shapes and connections at many levels.

Most leaders rise to the top for complex reasons rather than through either fortune or skill alone. This binary—fortune vs skill—rarely exists in pure form, but rather both in varying combinations. But we can compare these two methods of rising to the top of the oligarchy, by ability or fortune, using two contemporary examples—Henry Kravis and George W. Bush. Kravis, by diligent means and with great ability, rose from privilege to be one of the leaders of a financial empire and a member of leading networks, such as the Council on Foreign Relations and the Bilderberg Group. That which he had acquired with the thousand calculations in corporate takeovers, he kept with little trouble.

On the other hand, George W. Bush, nicknamed "shrub," inherited power from his father and grandfather. On acquiring an oil company, he lost it; on acquiring a baseball team, he ran it into the ground; and on becoming president, he did his best, with the aid of Vice President Cheney, to destabilize the financial underpinnings of the entire nation and most of the rest of the world by allowing unrestrained speculation in real estate and foreign adventures that benefited only a few cronies. It has even been speculated that the invasion of Iraq was associated with those family ties that we spoke of earlier in this chapter.

Further, by undermining historical alliances in Europe, Asia, and Latin America, Bush and his network nearly ruined a US foreign policy that had taken decades to build with the hard work and blood of many fine citizens. The US is still excavating itself from the fallout of Bush's operational antics.

Islamic State incursions throughout the world, the Syrian civil war that uprooted millions of people, and renewed conflicts with Russia are only the obvious results of the Bush administration's policies. At a deeper level, populism that disguises itself as nationalism, self-dealing by the Trump cabal, and the rush to a war footing to distract from the Trump administration's inexperience are also great risks to global stability. Immigration from damaged countries in the Middle East is destabilizing European nations just when policy coherence would help arrest climate change.

It should be noted, too, that the too-quick rise to power of the inexperienced Obama only exacerbated income inequality and the financial fragility of major economies. Obama was unable to rebuild firm financial conditions and effective regulation to stabilize society because he hadn't developed an understanding of them based on decades in politics. Efforts such as the Consumer Protection Agency, however, are well-meaning and formally sound, even though they have too little basis in the rest of the bureaucracy or support from financial institutions themselves. Again, an oligarch who has not built firm foundations may be able with great ability to lay them afterward, but it will be difficult for the architect and a danger to the building.

CHAPTER VIII: CONCERNING THOSE WHO HAVE RISEN TO THE OLIGARCHY BY WICKEDNESS

An oligarch may rise from a modest position in two other ways, neither of which can be entirely attributed to fortune or skill. These methods are when, by nefarious methods, the oligarch ascends to leadership, or when by the favor of fellow citizens, a private person becomes the leader of a faction. The first method can be illustrated by one example that should be sufficient. The second appears in the next chapter.

From the beginning, Putin and his circle sought to create an oligarchy ruled by a close-knit faction of ex-security officials and the managers of major state industries, using the form of democracy for decoration rather than direction. The leading oligarchs behind Boris Yeltsin's administration may have thought that Putin was not a threat and so allowed him to rise in the ranks. Once in control, his plans unfolded, and his group, using KGB methods, including poisoning detractors, took over state operations, doling out favors, offices, and contracts from the post-Soviet system while keeping the form of government in place. Using democratic form, while operating the state for the benefit of the few who received state largess, shows how relying on a form of government for their liberty can deceive a nation's citizens. Similar operations are emerging in the US and Turkey.

Formal government remains definitional. The point here is not to ignore form or pretend that form is irrelevant, but to recognize the limits of form, how it interacts with operational governance, and how form can be twisted to benefit a few even when constitutions are written for the "whole people." Written constitutions remain useful as placeholders defining expectations for leaders, managers, and the general public, but traditional and effective states such as Britain operate with a constitutional authority distributed across many acts of Parliament and court cases. France and Russia have had several constitutions as have other nations. The point is that the people thrive or suffer more according to the operations of government than its form.

Within a few years of the 1917 Russian revolution and the 1918 constitution that was ratified along with the *Declaration of Rights of The Working and Exploited People*, oligarchy was once again the operational mode under Lenin where he was first among equals, but even more so under Stalin who excelled at managing the informal connections that comprise an oligarchic network. Then, with the economy collapsing in 1989, the government, which we can now describe as a form and mode of operations, changed from the Soviet oligarchy to democratic civil oligarchy under Yeltsin to a democracy disguising a ruling oligarchy under Putin and his network. In terms of the well-being of the people, economic inequality under Putin continues to widen. (As a result of privatization begun under Yeltsin, the Gini coefficient has risen from under 30 to over 40 since the fall of the USSR.) The Russian oligarchy now looks increasingly like Stalin's regime as Putin increases control over the other nodes of the network.

Although operations are more difficult to understand, they are central to how the form of governance determines the well-being of the people. Operations, such as institutional interactions, are likely to be misunderstood because of their complexity. Even more opaque are those informal connections between individuals and groups where key strategic decisions are often negotiated and less popular decisions are made. The form of this book makes a fuller discussion of this issue difficult here.

As an aside, writers seeking to gain fame through their explanations of power will usually fall back on a discussion of form and the false equivalence of democracy with liberty. Further, discussion of form is vulnerable to appealing generalizations and tempts readers by subverting their psychology. It circumvents the more difficult task of understanding how multiple operations cause particular events, especially since a discussion of various contributory causes does not satisfy readers' need to identify with an essential explanation. Yet all ecosystems—biological, political, and psychological—are co-dependent and participate in multilevel evolution. The serious reader will excuse this assertion.

In practice, Putin's group appropriated funds that belonged to the Russian state, sent them to foreign banks, and reinvested them in Russia as, piece by piece, Yeltsin's regime failed. Putin's group illegally used repatriated state funds to purchase and take over the state apparatus. The civil oligarchy was replaced by ruling oligarchs—Gennady Timchenko, Vladimir Yakunin, Yury Kovalchuk, and Sergey Chemezov among others—with Putin as their leader, negating by subversion the broader franchise that had been building since Mikhail Gorbachev's leadership.

As with the US and EU, a large group of confusing regulations and contradictory laws means that at one level or another everybody is operating in violation of some law. Thus, any entity is liable at any time to be sued or arrested. Loose enforcement is all that prevents US leadership from attacking its enemies in court, although that restraint is disappearing with suits and police investigations against civil leaders such as Bill Clinton, George W. Bush, Obama, and Trump. Similar tactics have been used by competing oligarchs since the Roman Republic, subverting justice for gains by a small group. The Roman Republic cases are well documented.

The contradictory regulations are not a mistake, although they may arise from failure to coordinate actions across the network. They are an inherent mechanism, driven by legislative responses to the demands of specific interest groups, for keeping oligarchs aligned and using the same protocols for communication and concurrence. In a civil oligarchy, it reduces infighting, since one lawsuit produces another in response. If someone steps out of line, the security state can easily make their lives miserable, as Trump is discovering. These methods, learned from Napoleon and firmly established in the US by J. Edgar Hoover, increase legal control over uncooperative oligarchs. In Putin's case, direct governance by the oligarchs makes the legal system their personal tool. Trump acts in a complementary way with inherited money from the Koch brothers, the Bradley and Olin foundations, and others seeking similar controls in the US. US institutions, especially the courts, have so far been able to limit Trump's planned chaos better than the ruined institutions of Russia were able to control Putin. Whether the security apparatus and courts of the US remain a sufficient bulwark against autocracy is playing out in real time.

The Western security state usually controls activities on the edge of acceptability through an elite group that operates both on its own behalf and in collaboration with major industries such as pharmaceuticals, defense, transportation, heavy industry, technology, energy, communications, and agribusiness. Through state organs of control and links with media to promote their rhetoric of democratic form, the oligarchic network channels major initiatives, contracts, and tax revenues to allied industries, so long as they support the security state, help security officers maintain control of information resources, and keep tabs on rising alternative bases of power. The security state, for its part, privileges the corporations that support its controls. If Trump's apparent attack on the institutions of the security state at the beginning of his administration are more than a theatrical gesture, the security state may make it difficult for his regime to remain stable.

Under a similar model, a delicate balance of power exists between industrialists and the security state in Russia, the US, China, the EU, and to a lesser extent Indonesia and India in both civil and ruling oligarchies. Yet the reins of power are loosely held within a broad range, far wider than the people usually condone with their reliance on moral codes provided by the oligarchs themselves. Within the oligarchy everyone in the networks of power knows that they have to give to get. Sometimes the balance sways one way and sometimes another, but the majority of rich and powerful individuals, families, and clans remains in place through changing institutions unless a serious conflict among oligarchs interferes.

In Russia, the security state, led by Putin, won its conflict against global industrialists and took over the political state with illegal financial manipulations. In 2016, an alliance of conservatives, libertarians, and evangelical Christians seems to have defeated the neo-liberal globalists in the US using similar tactics of financial manipulation and voter suppression. The conservatives intend to return power to localities, which are more easily controlled by corporate largesse and cultures specific to geographical regions than the Federal government, which requires a bevy of expensive lobbyists to manage. Hence, the call for smaller government is code for greater control of the state by corporations and local oligarchs. The form of government has had little to do with the operations of the state in either case, the system of voting being subverted by outright deception about the true intentions of the new leadership. Voter suppression has been increasingly effective in eliminating millions of people of color, gender-based communities, students, the elderly, and citizens living overseas. In Colorado, for example, more than 19 percent of voters were scrubbed from registration lists. The free press, another oxymoron, has done little to thwart Trump by putting his picture on every front page every day throughout the campaign. The Libertarians, because their exciting adventures body slamming journalists and the like, sell newspapers better than the tired bureaucrats of the neoliberals.

Suddenly, rising supra-national initiatives, such as the EU and global trade agreements driven by financial interests, have been thwarted in their effort to create a planetary operating model. Natural resources corporations that now control the US and Russian governments, as well as Australia, Brazil, and most countries in the Middle East, have somewhat different interests than those corporations whose business is in the Internet and consumer products, or engineering globalists whose power is being reduced by isolationism in many jurisdictions. These international oligarchs also seek to reduce the power of nations, undermining the Peace of Westphalia, while increasing control by multinational financial corporations. Global interests will push back against the Trump administration's call for closed borders. These interests are shaping up to be the next major battle among oligarchs. We see globalist leaders such as Jamie Dimon speaking out in favor of greater support of precarious populations while the localist libertarians seek to exploit those groups.

Thus, the approaches promoted by neoliberal and conservative oligarchs drive power alternately to multinational organizations and local corporations. Climate change also pushes leaders to retrench locally when global conditions threaten states and corporations. Large land masses with smaller populations like Australia and Brazil are more easily controlled by agricultural and commodity oligarchs. Their smaller populations and less intrusive foreign policies reduce the need for a complex state security to maintain control of their people.

In Machiavelli's time, rulers were advised to closely examine all those injuries they needed to inflict on their people and to do them all at once to avoid repeating them daily. By not continually upsetting the people, they reassured productive citizens and won their allegiance with benefits, as in Venice and, intermittently, in Florence and Milan. In modern times, political and economic systems are too large and complex to avoid continual adjustments. Because of contemporary global interactions, Machiavelli's goal of securing the state can today only be accomplished by gradual change and permanent, low-level conflict justified through channels provided by corporate media.

CHAPTER VIII: CONCERNING THOSE WHO HAVE RISEN TO THE OLIGARCHY... 39

In the current situation, injuries cannot all be done at once, so that, being tasted less often, they offend less. Trump's continuous insults, and those of a generation of conservatives, increase the anxiety of citizens, making strong public relations more necessary to immobilize them. Contemporary leaders also distribute the perceived benefits to society little by little, so that the flavor of them may last longer and balance the continuous small injuries. This may also be a preferred method that was not fully realized in the sixteenth century as consistent with the complex workings of any state or organization. Those people outside oligarchic networks, whose skills are needed to run the state or the corporation, may be encouraged to support the oligarchy and build the technology that makes larger numbers of citizens dispensable. Yet many forces are at work and none of these effects are monolithic. Surplus citizens not needed for labor may threaten oligarchic control and necessitate further suppression of voting. Climate change may provoke a significant reduction in the human population at the same time as technology improves to increase it.

Contemporary oligarchs ought to live among their people, not in gated communities, so that no unexpected circumstances surprise them. If oligarchs are isolated from the people and the need for change occurs, harsh measures are often too late to be effective and mild ones will not help, since oligarchic obligations will not have been secured with local power brokers. Although in modern times electronic sensors make even remote leaders aware of changes in real time, marshalling forces to address a problem still takes days, if not weeks. Nevertheless, spinning the news often makes people imagine that what happened did not happen as they remember it, but happened otherwise. Those who need someone else's authority to hold any opinion are easily swayed not only by a leader's friendly face, but also by the anger and the terror promulgated daily among disenfranchised citizens.

One cannot easily, with fair dealing and without injury to others, satisfy these wicked oligarchs who foolishly seek civil discord to help acquire limitless money, security, and power. They concede nothing without a demand. Whatever the people will submit to without insurrection becomes the level of self-interest and control these oligarchs enforce and the license they allow their allies. These controls on the people and freedoms for oligarchic cohorts continue until the people resist with words, money, and arms. These oligarchs undermine government for personal benefit and create imbalanced societies. While the civil oligarchs discussed in the next chapter operate with some significant measure of this self-interest, these ruling oligarchs attempt to take control of government directly and primarily for their own benefit.

The people, on the other hand, are easily satisfied, since their objective is more limited than that of most oligarchs, the latter wishing gain for themselves, while the former only desire not to be oppressed. The people's self-interest can be easily blunted by popular culture managed by corporate media. The constant din of love songs, for example, advertises that one should embrace one's emotions and spontaneous action while the effective oligarch, while strenuously committed to clear goals and detailed planning, studiously avoids the risk of allowing his or her gut to do the thinking.

3: Regarding the Form of Oligarchies

CHAPTER IX: CONCERNING A CIVIL OLIGARCHY

When a citizen becomes a leader, not by naked self-interest or intolerable violence, but through selection by other oligarchs and through endeavors that win the favor of the people, this individual operates in a civil oligarchy. Neither genius nor fortune is necessary to win the laurels in a civil oligarchy. The key characteristics of a civil oligarch are a happy shrewdness and apparent sincerity. Civil oligarchy is the most common structure in Europe and North America where corporations dominate domestic politics and the property rights of all are protected by law.

Political office in a civil oligarchy is obtained by the support of affinity groups such as developers, idealists, natural resource owners, and bankers, as well as by notable deeds that win general approval. In the US, a person can become president through winning a war (Eisenhower), speaking well (Obama), media notoriety (Reagan and Trump), or having a character that appeals to many types of people (Clinton). In parliamentary systems, oligarchs have greater sway in a similar process. Behind this appeal, all leaders need some well-connected, rich backers to build a critical mass of voters and vote-controlling organizations, and to assure the people through media channels that they are controlled not by business and government, but by their electoral will. Aligning these different interests requires substantial political skill. The oligarchs themselves may rule for the gain of their faction and its network, but in a civil oligarchy, they do not rule as oligarchs.

Franklin Delano Roosevelt and George H. W. Bush are good examples of when powerful families lead as benefactors of the people.

When the current oligarchs are pressured by the demands of the people, calling for workers' rights, equal economic and political opportunity, and greater pay, they begin to tout the reputation and popular virtues of one of themselves. They make him or her a figurehead, and so protected by one of their own, they pursue their ambitions. The people, finding that they cannot resist well-organized oligarchs, also promote the reputation of one of their group to be defended by his authority, but they rarely are as well organized and effective. Most often, these conflicting currents elect a civil oligarch as a compromise.

A leader who obtains control by the assistance of oligarchs maintains power differently than those who rise with the aid of the people. The former finds himself with many associates who consider themselves the oligarch's equal. To retain their favor, the leader can use their network to manage the other oligarchs as long as most are mutually supportive.

But a leader who becomes powerful by popular favor finds himself leading alone with most prepared to obey him, except some who are envious, or of the other party seeking to undermine him. The oligarchy, never resting and always well connected, works to unseat or at least diminish the influence of the popular leader.

The popular leader, in turn, defends against combined oligarchic power by compiling a network from stable channels such as connecting to community leaders with historically strong associations. As mentioned, Trump's coalition seeks to mimic this populist style while working with nationalist oligarchs from the oil patch and evangelical churches at the expense of the workers and minorities. Simultaneously, Trump stimulates worker's fears, strokes their cultural biases, and stokes their anger through well-funded libertarian channels so that they continue to support him in spite of his actions against their interests. His strategy masks logical and functional contradictions as well as buffering managerial incompetence.

Populism results in a new coalition of groups, such as when the neoliberals under Carter, oligarchs such as the Trilateral Commission, and financial interests outside the Democratic party machine, all focused on globalization, and took over the Democratic Party from the New Deal coalition that the Viet Nam war had discredited. These leaders unwittingly paved the way for Reagan, because they reprioritized the interests of the people that had been the hallmark of the New Deal. Carter himself was an outlier who had built his coalition through channels other than the usual

Democratic Party local leaders. His nomination succeeded because the party process of nominating candidates through local leadership had been compromised by left-leaning forces, but even so, his association with the Trilateral Commission allowed globalist oligarchs to increase their power.

Another example is the Trump coalition of political conservatives in the Tea Party, evangelicals, business leaders, libertarian philanthropists, law and order groups, and militarists. This coalition's success occurs after decades of libertarian network building by the Koch brothers, Scaife, and others already mentioned, developing conservative dominance at the local level in the majority of jurisdictions, and with an influx of funds from national organizations associated with fossil fuels, income protection, and nativism. Note that pseudo-populists, like Trump and Recep Tayyip Erdoğan, complicate this distinction with multiple deceptions that, even when revealed, fail to convince their followers of the duplicity of their leader. These false populist leaders operate quite differently than genuine populists like Juan Perón and Hugo Chávez.

As all oligarchs ceaselessly plan to control hearts and wallets, the civil oligarch must actively curry favor within various networks or else lose power. The worst that a civil oligarch may expect from a hostile people is to be abandoned by them when they retreat into their communities apart from government. The people's organizations are not cohesive, but are rather factionalized by identity politics that corporate media attempt to coopt by appealing to elements of identity in the news, fiction, and advertising. At the same time these groups' identities are fervently protected by their adherents against the state and corporation, acting as a sort of sanctuary for those who are truly oppressed and who suffer from disenfranchisement on many levels.

From hostile oligarchs, however, the civil oligarch has to fear not only abandonment, but also insurgence and betrayal, since they are already organized to do so. On the other hand, while the civil oligarch is compelled to live with the same people, allied oligarchs can be replaced, because an oligarch is able to make and unmake alliances. Hence, we see some civil oligarchs who, when threatened, seek extraordinary powers, like the aforementioned Erdoğan, who must avoid the military oligarchs of Turkey removing him from power. In a corporate example, Gates created a new alliance with Buffet, allowing some of his technology and conservative political alliances to deteriorate. Trump made new alliances with Libertarians, Conservatives, and Evangelicals, forsaking his alliances with Democrats and moderates to win the presidency.

In another example, Obama made new alliances with the oil cartel by opening up the Arctic to drilling by Shell, allowing his relations with environmentalists to deteriorate. The oil cartel and its supporters in Congress then, when given an inch, tried to destroy the Environmental Protection Agency. In turn, Obama supported environmentalism in the Paris talks. This mercurial behavior shows that channels of networks have complex flows and can easily be bidirectional and intermittent rather than a guarantee of power. The oligarch must be cautious when shifting alliances since there may be unintended consequences, as Trump found out with his initiative to repeal the Affordable Care Act, more popularly known as Obamacare. Further, a civil leader may not give or take away authority when it pleases him, even with executive power, because every other oligarch has independent assets and power bases. So, civil oligarchs constantly need to placate other oligarchs, while representing the people in a more rudimentary fashion.

Therefore, to make this point clearer, civil oligarchs ought to be looked at mainly in two ways. They may elect one of their group as a leader, as in the Politburo Standing Committee of the Communist Party of China and as in Singapore. Or they may continue to rule as a group without an individual leading personality, as in the EU. Both systems operate effectively when adapted to local culture.

Income and asset inequality persist between classes and lead to emphasizing economic determinism. The top 0.1 percent of earners worldwide has gained far more since the Great Recession than any other class even though those same bankers, mortgage initiators, and hedge-fund managers' actions led to the financial collapse of 2007–2008. From this fact, we see that economic forces are powerful and governments by comparison are weak, and that conservative and libertarian efforts continue to diminish the reach of central governments. Economic determinants operate throughout oligarchic networks, and one is tempted to essentialize economic determinism.

Nevertheless, power is not determined solely by money. Cultural forces already cited, environmental factors, chance, and other conditions of opportunity challenge economic power at all points along the path. Yet productive people continue to seek the apparent security of wealth to reinforce their position against misfortune. The establishment of a figurehead who can stand in for wealth, with whom both the people and the other oligarchs can identify, often turns out to be a stable alternative to oligarchs governing for themselves. The civil oligarch is supported by many committees of both oligarchs and the people who, even while disagreeing, sustain the administration through adherence to the laws of the state and principles of honorable opposition, which means they do not seek to kill him outright.

In either case, those civil leaders who are not rapacious ought to be honored. Those who continue to grasp for wealth and power even when they have enough themselves may be looked at in two ways. They may do this through pusillanimity, distraction, and anxiety, in which case a strong oligarch ought to make use of them, especially those who are good counsellors. That way, while prospering, strong leaders honor themselves, and in adversity do not fear these bureaucrats. On the other hand, when, for their own ambition or ideology (and ideology is rarely honorably sustained), bureaucrats avoid binding themselves to traditional oligarchic organizations, it is a token that they are giving more thought to themselves than to their roles and responsibilities. In adversity those focused too avidly on seeking acceptance always help to ruin the leader.

Those who become oligarchs through the favor of the workers or the citizens ought to keep them friendly. This is easy to do since the people only ask not to be ruined by him. But one, who in opposition to the people becomes an oligarch, like Mitt Romney, primarily through the favor of the other oligarchs, should, above all, seek to win over the people or employees. This may easily be done by taking them under oligarchic protection by increasing wages and providing benefits rather than pointing out their weaknesses in a derogatory manner. Receiving what they had hoped for when they were expecting evil, people are bound more closely to their benefactor. Thus, the people quickly become devoted to the oligarch who is not transparently malicious, although popular culture, especially the ubiquitous movies about revenge and conspiracy, have made many people anxious to bring down others if for no other reason than to satisfy their resentment. Liberal leaders in Hollywood and elsewhere should remember that a cultural leader reaps what he sows.

As mentioned above, an oligarch can win the people's affections in many ways, but since these ways vary circumstantially, one cannot provide fixed rules, although the cliché of bread and circuses often suffices. Besides benefits and entitlements, there are also cultural supports such as laws for treating unwanted pregnancies that permit abortion, balanced treatment of crimes, religious and civil rights, careful attitudes toward war until you are in one (whereupon the opposite is helpful), advantages in business, and other rights and privileges that make it apparently supportive of the people's moral positions. It is useful for an oligarch to keep the people friendly; otherwise there is no security in adversity.

President Clinton, for example, sustained the attack of Congressional Republicans, conservative funders, and religious leaders during the Lewinsky affair. Against them, he was defended by his supporting oligarchs, his administration, and the voters. To overcome his impeachment, it was only necessary to secure himself against a few, but this would have been insufficient had the voters been hostile. And do not let anyone impugn this statement with the trite proverb that "He who builds on the people, builds on the mud." This is true only when a private citizen imagines a popular foundation, persuading himself that the people will free him when he is oppressed by the oligarchy. In this impression, he would find himself often deceived, as happened to the Gracchi in Rome. The futures of Trump, Nigel Farage, Marine Le Pen, and other nationalist leaders will unfold.

Given a civil oligarch who is established, who can work with other oligarchs, who appears to keep faith with the people, even if only keeping faith with some of them, and is a person of courage, undismayed in adversity, and willing to change positions when circumstances change, who, by resolution and energy, keeps the people encouraged, such a one will never find himself overwhelmed by circumstances. Through such complex skills, civil oligarchy succeeds; no single talent is sufficient for sustainability.

Civil oligarchies are endangered when they transition from a civil to a ruling oligarchy, as Trump's administration appears to be trending toward, or to a military form of government as attempted by Richard Nixon's clique with its organized crime affiliations. Such a change was also attempted by Cheney with his business partners in the oil patch and the military. Such groups either rule personally, through fear, or through the courts. In the latter case their government is weaker and more insecure because it relies entirely on those who are raised through the judiciary to agree with a professed ideology. These judges, especially in troubled times, can destroy the administration with great ease, as they did with Nixon, either by intrigue or open defiance. There have been several recent instances how a cadre of liberal judges raised the ire of oligarchs, such as in Turkey. Now Erdoğan, under legitimate pressure from the Syrian civil war, Kurdish rebels, and Russian incursions, seeks to elect 50 percent of the judiciary to reduce their ability to contradict his dictates.

Contemporary conservative power brokers seek to gain adherents in courts at all levels and teach conservative lawyers how to win judgeships. Nixon, for example, would have taken over the government had he passed S1 and built his network with stronger connections to other power bases, but he was isolated by his lack of what we have called the happy shrewdness that Clinton and others wielded with aplomb.

When a ruling oligarch like Trump or Putin takes over from a civil oligarchy, the opposing parties, such as the Democratic Party's leadership in the US or Khodorkovsky's group in Russia, may not be sufficiently organized to exercise authority amid the tumult. This situation is true under chaotic conditions at all levels. Citizens and employees, accustomed to receiving interpretations of laws from presidents and judges, or corporate strategy filtered through human resources departments, are not trained to obey political leaders who have been removed from power or middle managers amid confusion. These citizens or employees, through jealousy of those immediately above them, maintain connections to their top leaders, as seen with populists like Perón or Theodore Roosevelt. Therefore, when taking over from a civil oligarchy, a ruling oligarch must be prepared to rule 24-seven and to both love and need constant feedback. This need has become both Trump's strength and weakness.

There will always be in doubtful times a scarcity of men and women that the magistrates and the workers can trust. The ruling oligarch cannot rely on what is observed in quiet times, when citizens have little need of the state and vice versa, because then everyone agrees. They all promise. When death is distant, they all wish to take one for the team, but in troubled times, when the state has need of its citizens, a ruling oligarch finds few willing to sacrifice. Experimenting with loyalty is decidedly dangerous because it often fails. Therefore, a wise oligarch ought to adopt a strategy that links citizens to the administration, and then followers will more often remain faithful.

The popular notion of the oligarch as a leader only in financial matters should not cloud our understanding of the reach of oligarchy through nearly all forms of power in all times. Even in civil oligarchies, the notion that an oligarch is only a financial leader and subject to the law as a higher form of governance, and that oligarchs have agreed to be subject to law that protects their property rights, must be propagated to gain adherence of the people, but is largely illusory.

The argument that you are only an oligarch when very, very rich ignores the ubiquity of oligarchic domination and the reach of oligarchic networks beyond finance through institutions of all sorts to all aspects of control. Neither is oligarchy simply elitism, since elites are constantly changing, and elitism is psychologically solipsistic and logically redundant.

Oligarchs agree to obey the law because they have directly or indirectly influenced its making through their networks. They protect their property in civil oligarchies at the outset of a regime through establishing constitutional law, that is, the law by which the operations of the state are governed, and also through civil, criminal, tax, tort, real estate, intellectual property, and other laws. The law is made by oligarchs directly when they act in legislative office. They also enforce laws or make them indirectly when their agents, either paid or agreed in principle, moral code, and mutual benefit, do so.

In some networks, property rights are protected by law while civil rights are not. Singapore's Prime Minister Lee Kuan Yew insisted that all oligarchs follow the rule of law and developed a civil oligarchy from a corrupt postcolonial system. In several important legal cases in Singapore, top oligarchs were forced to pay heavily for corrupt practices. In one instance involving Tan Kia Gan (1966), Prime Minister Lee forced his colleague, Tan, off the board of Malaysia Airways for bribery regarding the purchase of Boeing airplanes, establishing a rule of law against the expectation that bribing officials secured a transaction. In the case of Minister of National Development Teh Cheang Wan (1986), bribery charges resulted in Teh's suicide, showing how traditional culture also propagates through the network. Lee showed that property rights can be protected by strict rule of law and people can be forced to obey without giving them significant civil rights. Oligarchs should note that such rule of law does not have to be enforced perfectly, only predictably, and with some consistency. Oligarchs have been endlessly inventive in protecting property in all forms of governance.

Oligarchs must work together for a consistent culture throughout the state and corporation or conflict ensues to the detriment of all. When people rise up against financial oppression, the loss of their civil rights, or their support is needed in times of war, oligarchs must make laws more in the interest of the majority. During the New Deal and immediately after WWII, Western leaders needed to make capitalism seem more favorable than communism to the people, but even then, oligarchs operated in their own interest, albeit with smaller margins. Management and employees mutually benefit through labor relations in which wages and security are increased for workers, while owners still profit immensely and can, when pressed, revoke pension agreements. The real difficulties arise when oligarchs' interests differ, such as in the conflicts between renewable energy and fossil fuels, between agricultural landowners and industrialists in the US Civil War, between religious sects in the Thirty Years' War, and currently between internationalists and nationalists in the US and EU. In these situations, law becomes a tool for one oligarchic group to use against another. Oligarchs may compromise or else divergence and warfare erupts to the detriment of the state and corporation. Without compromise, divergence changes society.

An example of diverse and divergent interests working together, through a civil oligarchy, can be found in laws decriminalizing youth and youth activity in recent years in the US. The liberal organization, the American Civil Liberties Union, challenged the "school-to-prison pipeline," a disturbing national trend where children are funneled out of public schools and into the juvenile and criminal justice system. Many of these children have learning disabilities or histories of poverty, abuse, and neglect, and would benefit from additional educational and counseling services. Instead, they are isolated, punished, and pushed out of the educational system. "Zero-tolerance" policies lead to students being criminalized for minor infractions of school rules that would have been handled inside the school in decades prior. Students of color are especially vulnerable to these push-out trends and the discriminatory application of discipline.

Conservatives had long promoted such "zero tolerance" policies, but some Christians like former Nixon hatchet man Chuck Colson emerged from prison believing that the church should minister to prisoners. Born-again Christians such as Colson and the Republican leader of the California Assembly, Pat Nolan, imprisoned for taking bribes, felt that the ethic of forgiveness should be reinstated as a key plank in the Christian religio-political platform. Liberals, reaching across the aisle, and academic researchers pointed out that it was far less expensive to treat juvenile offenders and counsel them and their families than to pay for more jails.

This coalition of Christian and liberal groups engaged conservative leaders like the American Legislative Exchange Council, heavily funded by the Koch brothers, and stalwarts Grover Norquist, the anti-tax campaigner, and Newt Gingrich, former Speaker of the House, convincing them that the combination of Christian values and cost benefit justified decriminalizing youth behavior. This conservative network connected to the ACLU and liberal campaign lawyers to change the laws in many states. Expanding prison reform to a broader population, conservatives argued that keeping mandatory minimums for felony drug offenders drives up prison costs while doing little to enhance public safety. Given the undeniable costs, the dubious benefits of mass, long-term incarceration of nonviolent drug offenders, and Christian ideals, the network encouraged state legislators to give judges more flexibility in sentencing youthful offenders.

Texas, North Carolina, Nebraska, and Utah are among the states that have benefited from the expanded network of liberal and conservative campaigners for different reasons—cost, forgiveness, and social justice—to the same effect. In September of 2015, ALEC and the National Black Caucus of State Legislators formed a new partnership to prioritize the prevention of overcriminalization, the reforming of mandatory minimum sentencing laws, the reduction of recidivism rates, and the promotion of community-based alternatives to lengthy jail stays for non-violent offenders. ALEC and NBCSL also developed a shared statement of principles on criminal justice reform that will guide members' efforts in state outreach and education in spite of different principles and beliefs. Not all network affiliations achieve such potentially broad benefits, but these details of network building clarify the processes of network building and social change. Jeff Sessions, however, has recently reinstated the war on drugs, undermining this useful alliance.

Chapter X: Concerning the Ways That the Strength of Oligarchies Ought to Be Measured

An important characteristic of oligarchies is whether a group has enough power that, in case of need, it can support itself with its own resources, or whether it always relies on the assistance of others. Specifically, strong oligarchs can, with an abundance of friendly, wealthy citizens in domestic and global financial dealings, supportive employees in expanding or defending a business, or money of their own, hire sufficient lawyers, lobby enough sympathetic government officials, or raise an army to engage anyone opposing them in a deal or in a war. Those who cannot protect themselves on the relevant field of encounter are forced to defend their positions by delaying and avoiding conflict and have difficulty taking the initiative when opportunity knocks. Pure types, either strong or weak in all respects, however, hardly exist in today's interdependent world. This point clarifies how networks operate both as a whole and in parts as subnets as was notable in the networking associated with the alliance of liberals and conservatives in the example of the treatment of youthful offenders in the prior chapter.

Political postures, associated with power ranging from strength to intelligence to security, link national and corporate networks to individual impulses and apply individual psychology to how large organizations operate. An oligarch can use false equivalences to gain like-minded adherents with claims such as that the budget of a country with its own currency ought to balance like a household budget. In some ways, however, the global system does work like the individual's self-image. Individual organisms, corporations, and nations are all too intricate and tied together for true independence, ultimately operating best through mutual aid as the wise oligarch knows. Even the strongest organizations must focus their assets in some areas while deferring action in others. Oligarchs prioritize their values with policy and take advantage of the moment without sacrificing long-term advantage. Detailed negotiations among mutually supportive oligarchs are rarely visible to history, but effective plans reflect their agreements.

All people negotiate around priorities. Every day we get up and decide what's important to do. But can we really generalize across the whole set of decision-making bodies from powerful oligarchies to communities to families to individuals faced with threats and fears? Understanding similarity at different scales in politics helps clarify environmental issues for specialists and planners. But communicating to the general public what decisions are unique at each scale and what are common across two or more levels might best be subordinated to binaries that reflect individual psychology. Transparency is the better approach where possible, but not if it creates confusion and makes complex operations more difficult and confusing.

Difficulties arise in making decisions that display the strength or weakness of organizations. Small groups need consistent goals and procedures, equal group involvement and commitment, methods to reduce conflict, strong communication and literacy skills, related communication styles, equal power, good memory of the group's past, and strong inter-group associations. These practices strengthen small nations and businesses, communities, and families.

Large, heterogeneous groups inevitably marshal their forces more slowly. They must expect a wider range of results. Nevertheless, the sensible oligarch sees relationships and measures how much force must be applied to each decision, including its implications for other decisions, strategy, and specific actions, to maximize its chances of success. It is safer, at first, to consider various choices heuristically, modeling with an eye toward how channels between companies and countries operate. Such abstractions and models about the complexity of action are important because some oligarchs maintain publicly that they are convinced by the delusions of independence and personal freedom, while close examination shows that these are marginal situations in our interdependent relationships, organizations, and the biosphere.

We must also question whether negotiation should be considered a kind of conflict as some business schools teach, or whether war, as Carl von Clausewitz maintains, is a kind of negotiation. The oligarch, while proselytizing Darwin's imperialist idea of competition, must also understand the ubiquity of complex commensal organizations from governance to interactions in the biosphere. Finally, with regard to networks, we must ask to what degree an oligarchic network can operate independently. Smaller subnets may be effective if they have enough linkages to other sources of wealth and power through trade and common culture. England, for example, is about to learn whether Brexit will make it vulnerable to attacks on its currency, like George Soros' in the early 1990s. Large corporations also moderate their differences with a combination of competition and cooperation. All large technology firms promote the idea of coopetition to executives, research, sales, and marketing employees to help them understand why negotiation remains more important to success under more conditions than the emotionally satisfying confrontation and total victory promoted in the media.

In the case of weaker firms, where an owner must be prepared to take greater risks, one can say little more than to encourage such oligarchs to lawyer-up, hedge all bets, and avoid defending a lawsuit if possible. *Gawker* could have settled with Hulk Hogan promptly and saved its bacon. Whoever hedges equity well and manages the employee concerns as stated above will be able to defend against competition and a hostile takeover, for CFOs are always averse to enterprises where problems can be easily seen. It's difficult to attack an organization whose equity is well positioned or has a poison pill in place and is not hated by its employees or citizens.

The oil field service companies of the US and Europe are well fortified by having supportive regulators, who are also often ex-employees; tax advantages negotiated by lobbyists; and a high barrier to entry from new enterprises. They also have private armies, such as Halliburton's KBR, to defend their positions around the world. They even use their mercenaries to support national armies, such as in Iraq. They have ex-employees in Congress, the courts, regulatory bodies, the cabinet, and even in the vice presidency. Their price-to-book ratio is quite low compared to, say, tech companies, even when oil prices plummet.

CHAPTER X: CONCERNING THE WAYS THAT THE STRENGTH OF OLIGARCHIES... 53

The oil field service companies act like political parties. Koch Industries holds annual meetings to establish policy for all US conservatives that ultimately support their own businesses. They are obedient to nations only when it suits them, or they are forced to by other members of the energy sector. They do not fear other competing powers because they are fortified by their national and global connections in such a way that everyone thinks that attacking them financially, legally, or by regulation would be tedious and difficult, since they have influence in legislatures, regulatory bodies, and the courts. They fund academic institutions and think tanks to promote their ideas. They always keep enough cash and other assets in private depots for support in tough times. Beyond this, to keep their people satisfied and without loss to their corporations, they strengthen local communities by providing jobs.

Therefore, a company that has a strong asset base and enough adherents to its cultural and religious roots cannot be easily attacked. If anyone attacks, they will be beaten in the courts or through public relations and the press, in Congressional Committees, or in quiet regulatory meetings where often a word or a gesture is enough to quell opposition. You might retort: If someone owns property exposed to the enemies of the oil field service companies and sees it attacked either legally or financially, they will not remain loyal. We answer that a powerful and courageous oil field service oligarch like Cheney or Charles Koch will overcome short-term difficulties by assuring his employees and backers that no danger will long endure, or by nurturing fear of their enemy's cruelty, or by spreading disinformation about climate change. This point of view becomes increasingly valid, if you remember that many conservatives, like alt-right, evangelical, and Islamic State partisans, vote, proselytize, and function against their self-interest in support of their culture and network.

To advance its interest an enemy might start a lawsuit, regulatory action, competitive incentives, or offer a new product or service such as solar energy to ruin an oil field service firm's good deal. But just as the spirits of these oligarchs' adherents—workers, associated oligarchs, or partners—are low, since oil prices are low and profits weak, Trump has installed the ex-CEO of Exxon, Rex Tillerson, as Secretary of State to insure the interests of fossil fuels are served by the state. In this way you can see how, Charles Koch's funding of conservative electoral victories in selected districts in Michigan, Ohio, and Pennsylvania has been vindicated as a winning tactic. Koch even appears not to have provisioned Trump's candidacy, supporting Trump's campaign assertions of political independence, while guaranteeing many libertarian cabinet seats in the Trump administration.

The employees of the oil companies and the other oligarchs, perceiving the state under obligation to them, expect increases in fossil fuel prices, for it is the nature of an oligarch to be bound by the benefits conferred as much as by those received. Therefore, if the ecology of networks is fully considered, it is apparent how an attentive oligarch links the minds of workers, associates, and confreres to keep them steadfast from first to last. That said and in due consideration of the big picture, the days of the global sway of fossil fuel oligarchs are numbered, because the power of solar cells, through organic perovskite or other new materials, wind power, and other alternative energy sources will eventually be realized due to climate change and the real cost of fossil fuel extraction.

In summary, the strength of an organization can be measured by internal and external levels of skill, planning and execution capability, and flexibility and logistics. Cash flows and other assets, supply chains, allies, environmental conditions, and culture internal, adjacent, and remote all play roles as network nodes and flows. We can, however, read a strong balance sheet one year and find a new technology ruins its predictive power the next. When feeling strongest and most secure, the far-sighted oligarch then looks for risks and threats. Asserting the primacy of a single kind of strength, hard or soft power, bold assertion or quiet diplomacy, misses the need to address different kinds of problems differently in personal, political, and planetary networks and their components. Strength is measured both tactically and strategically, giving and taking, through both short and long term.

Chapter XI: Concerning Ecclesiastical Oligarchies

It only remains now to speak of ecclesiastical oligarchies. Most difficulties in these offices occur prior to gaining a position of power. Once in control ecclesiastical oligarchs maintain their power by the laws and hierarchy of religion, as well as adherents' belief, which has a powerful hold on people and may be sustained no matter how their priests and pastors behave. Even when these oligarchs live immoral lives, their situation is usually secure. Problems occur only when they are exposed in the press and criminal courts. Perversions, like pederasty among Catholic priests, violent crimes, like those committed by Tony Alamo, Wayne Bent, Warren Jeffs, and Ervil LeBaron, and non-violent crimes like those committed by Jim Bakker, Kent Hovind,

L. Ron Hubbard, and other religious figures may make even the faithful pause.

Ecclesiastics have political organizations called congregations, but do not defend them, because preaching the word of their god markets their authority. They have subjects and workers, but do not rule them, since belief frees the faithful from care. Their holy artifacts, although unguarded, are usually not taken from them. These oligarchs by profession are well connected to their communities, since their responsibility is to comfort their congregations and accept voluntary donations and prescriptive tithes. They are in most nations free to speak out on any subject of interest to their followers, but they are not taxed. Such oligarchs are secure and happy although they present stern faces. Since they are upheld by forces that the human mind does not seek to change, we shall speak no more of them, because they are exalted and maintained by belief. It would be the act of a presumptuous and rash writer to criticize them especially in these days of religious revival in many parts of the world as Hillary Clinton and the satirists at Charlie Hebdo discovered.

Nevertheless, we should ask how religions have attained such great temporal power in Christianity, Islam, Judaism, Buddhism, and Hinduism since their descent after the Enlightenment. We point to the recent US and Indian elections, the expansion of the Islamic State, Israeli influence on the US Congress and in the situation in Palestine, Iranian nuclear ambitions, and other notable secular events, the terms of which have been determined by religious leaders, Israeli protestations of secular democracy within a Jewish state notwithstanding. Even now, presidents and prime ministers tremble before these religions. Trump has even proposed to free tax-exempt religious organizations to lobby despite the US Constitution, which prohibits the formation of a state religion.

One of the probable causes of religious resurgence may be traced to global communications media, starting as early as the nineteenth century telephone and telegraph and extending to contemporary Internet applications. Many civil and ethical issues in developed and wealthy countries are now dominated by a hypervigilance toward security and deviation in individual behavior, stimulated by communications technologies, resulting in a rigid and volatile moral and emotional climate. Social media consumers mirror the ecclesiastical temperament and its ancient moral codes, which filter relations between citizens through fixed beliefs and allegorical emotions rather than through the self-interest in and acknowledgement of diverse conditions that theories of rational actors in economics and politics predict. Trolls disrupt normal communications by exacerbating differences in a way that would have been suppressed by law if they were physically acting out their attacks. Ecclesiastical oligarchs understand how to manipulate people's inherent misconceptions about their surroundings that religions promote, such as the desire that there be a higher reality beyond the suffering of day-to-day life. They know, too, how to accent differences between individuals and groups to reinforce beliefs.

Outside of religious certainties, theories are constantly brought into question by new facts, and facts are often revealed as a type of belief that is only true in one theory. Classical mechanics, settled science for more than a century, was overturned in the last century. The classical economics of rational actors has been updated to behavioral economics. These behavioral models seem to be doing a better job of explaining economic activity than the classical economics of Adam Smith, who might have titled his opus *The Wealth of Oligarchs*. Yet religion is different in that it is not subject to being disproved like science. While they may be broken apart, as the Roman Church was by Martin Luther, or Hinduism was by Gautama Buddha, religions are typically stable. Religions may fragment over small differences, family, or corruption, but they rally over time.

This seemingly stable, but factional, state of theology can be understood by viewing humanity as part of a single complex entity that includes the biosphere. Religions, like species of animals and plants, change through divergence. They interact directly and indirectly via difference more than similarity. Otherwise, Jews, Christians, and Muslims would support each other, because they relate within their faith's so similarly. Their forms of worship separate them. For example, Roman Catholics believe that the wine used during the Eucharist actually transforms into the blood of Christ while Orthodox Christians believe that transubstantiation is metaphoric. Their common sacred lineage through Abraham appears to be forgotten as they allow colonialism and economics to antagonize them. How they function, between their people and institutions, is not a source of provocation.

Islamic banks are derived from the principles of the Koran, but have existed almost exclusively in the twentieth and twenty-first centuries associated with the revival of Islamic culture. Islamic banks share risk and reward with the borrower rather than charge a fixed rate of interest. In real-estate transactions, the bank buys property from the seller and then resells it at a profit to the buyer, payable in installments. The form of banking is somewhat different from Western banking, but the operations still create a profit for the bank.

New conditions, however, whether political circumstances, scientific inventions, or environmental changes, modify form and operations. The form of government changed with the American Revolution. A monarchy became a democracy. Instead of rule by an inherited aristocracy, a group of elected citizens governed the state. These citizens represent the oligarchy or in some cases offices are held by the oligarchs themselves. The operations of government such as tax collection, national defense, and responsibility for the well-being of the people remained in the hands of a few individuals, with benefits distributed more widely.

Moveable type, gunpowder, and semiconductors changed the operations of society. The length of the beaks of the overall population of Galapagos finches' change as annual rainfall rates change, with more finches with longer beaks surviving in dry years. If the rate of rainfall changes within a narrow range, the form of the beaks fluctuates, changing little over longer durations. But if changes in rainfall persist year after year, those birds whose beaks are adapted to new conditions will dominate, because they get more food than the birds with poorly adapted beaks. The plants, favored as food sources by certain varieties of finch, change in their distribution as well. In this way, to accommodate the new conditions that are beginning to appear with climate change, oligarchs must be prepared to address environmental changes by adjusting how they operate within the form of governance, using new technology and more adaptive political forms rather than attempting to revert to outdated technologies or to monarchy.

This environmental model, which treats politics, technology, and ecology similarly, shows that an oligarch can manage how individuals adapt while maintaining control over surplus and behavior. It must be clear, however, even to the most intransigent, that changing conditions require adaptation if you want to maintain control. A new technology like electric transport replaces internal combustion engines, but access to resources remains in the hands of a few, if different, individuals.

Ecclesiastical oligarchs can use religion to suppress and stimulate believers' fears to maintain control over them and to help them adapt in desirable directions. Religion helps oligarchs manage resources within the community, especially when times are hard as when dry conditions cause crop failures. Whatever the difficulty, ecclesiastical oligarchs maintain control over the faithful through using their need for social interaction. Believers come together, overlooking small internal differences, yet not without some grumbling that ecclesiastics learn how to suppress.

You may view this small set of examples as metaphoric, and that would be consistent with prior literary strategies of political writing. If, on the other hand, you accept a complex, rather than a linear, model, then these examples are not simply metaphoric, but show how similar forms of life at different scales and even on different levels of reality—psychic, political, economic, historical, scientific—operate similarly. These correspondences, then, if you are prepared to accept separating the operations of political life from the form of politics, simply reflect the facts as they present themselves, moment to moment in our minds, daily in our experience, and over longer durations in psychological, social, seasonal, evolutionary, and geologic time scales. Thus, as an oligarch, you seek to shape the divergences occurring at various locations and times, as well as those changes occurring within expected ranges, accommodated by any form of governance, by rebalancing assets and your workers' and citizens' roles.

Pope Francis, like his namesake, attempts to rebalance the Roman Catholic social contract with the faithful by strengthening people's awareness of the condition of the poor and needy. In *Laudato Si'*, the Pope links the teaching of Jesus to environmentalism and calls on political leadership to rebalance both the environment and the social contract. At the same time, the gods and institutions of evangelical Christians, Zionist Jews, and fundamentalist Hindus and Muslims increasingly appear as the direct agents of political reaction.

From a slightly different viewpoint, contemporary reigniting of religion and ecclesiastical oligarchies must be associated with human adaptation to modern technologies, an increase of individual power, and the heightened availability of information, weapons, and communication. People feel empowered by inventions, software, and advertising to satisfy their individual desires. Yet, this religious renaissance appears after several centuries of the suppression of religion in many nations. Several other causes are important to consider. The focus of Germany and Europe in general on the Jewish religion during WWII resulted in the state of Israel, which, along with Pakistan, became one of the first important religious states in modern times. Many other state religions have since been established, notably Islam in Iran. Saudi Arabia, like the Vatican, is an ancient ecclesiastical oligarchy. US Christians also seek to establish a state religion, even though the US Constitution expressly forbids it.

Other state religions have followed the example of those in Israel and Pakistan, including Islamic State. The institution of Sharia law, evangelical Christianity, new age philosophy, and deep ecology all appear as important counter-revolutions to the Enlightenment. All of them, including deep ecology, seek to change the relationship between the individual and the group, undermining humanist individualism. Yet ecclesiastical oligarchies continue to reinforce economies where power operates quietly within a well-defended state, corporation, or self. In some secular states, too, secret groups and hidden connections direct the culture of leadership. A good example is the US government that derives from Benjamin Franklin's penchant for clustered secret societies, where distributed groups are controlled by a centralized secret assembly that is itself secret from the distributed ones. This strategy continues in the present day through concentric organizations, driven by both new and inherited wealth as we have pointed out already.

These shadowy organizations encourage factionalism and emphasize the binaries that separate the citizen from the world. They support individual identities that mimic how an oligarch divides the world and the network, juxtaposed against the mass of isolated individuals, who are thereby more easily managed. Repression of organized labor, promotion of technologies focused on individuals like cellphones and the social media of manufactured identities, and communications emphasizing individual choice methodically break down traditional communities and other intermediate institutions between the state and the individual.

Such an oligarchy, shaping the individual, society, and even the way we look at the biosphere, drives the renaissance of religious and related conservative networks. Increased oligarchic control of commerce, combined with social media, strips power from intermediate institutions of all stripes.

Corporate culture abstracts people's needs, the headache from the chemistry that causes it and loneliness from the destruction of institutions that would otherwise assist people. It fails to offer the comfort that religion delivers to the sick and sick of heart, as well as to those excluded minorities and individuals who make up the majority of the human population. Religion includes the faithful and allows them expertise denied by meritocracy. No wonder conservatives win evangelical votes.

Until and unless corporate and state secular configurations provide appropriate support to people in difficulty and to those striving to improve themselves beyond big bank accounts, asset building focused on accumulation of capital will not eliminate the need of the underclasses for religions and states. Disheartened, they cleave to religion and other belief-based institutions through fields of promises. Witness how, in a few short years, the US electorate was convinced to forgot how *laissez-faire*, pro-corporate policies caused the economies of the world to crash in 2007. People cling to those religions offering salvation and community since individuals do not thrive alone.

Most corporations and states have not understood these religious revivals or effectively engaged the problems they pose. They assume that they need not address these issues to achieve their personal leadership goals. Although politicians promise policies to appease the values of religions, such as limiting abortion, they have been content for religion to increase its mindshare without realizing that corporatism depends on a rationality that conflicts with the appeal of religious faith. These religions are already beginning to bite the corporate hand that feeds them. Yet, even in Christianity, Pauline oligarchic tendencies are being undermined by Pope Francis' appeal to constituencies beyond the front pews.

4: On Managing Assets within Organizations

CHAPTER XII: HOW MANY KINDS OF ASSETS, WORKERS, AND SOLDIERY THERE ARE, AND CONCERNING CONSULTANTS AND LOBBYISTS

Having examined the characteristics of oligarchies and their networks, it remains to discuss the means of control via their assets, adherents, and policies.

An oligarchy must have well-laid foundations and connections. Otherwise it will quickly collapse under predictable pressures from other groups with competing interests. The chief foundations of all states and companies, new and old as well as composite, are good laws and regulations, good methods of managing assets, adherents, and policies, and many bilateral and multi-lateral alliances. While there cannot be good laws and regulations when the oligarchy is not well stocked provisions and managed, it does not follow that, when well provisioned, it will always have balanced policies, laws, and regulation. We must therefore discuss oligarchic laws and regulations, as well as communications, armaments, and other assets.

The assets and adherents of an oligarch are either owned, rented, or paid from predictable cash flows. The absence of banks increases volatility in a way that threatens both commerce and the well-being of citizens and workers. Banks, especially central banks, manage the system of credit by which trade is conducted and war is waged. Banks must keep economies balanced by avoiding burdening populations with debt, while at the same time making money available by issuing those debt instruments.

© The Author(s) 2018
J. Sherry, *The Oligarch*, DOI 10.1007/978-3-319-62169-2_4

Unequal wealth is one of the chief concerns of any oligarch, who understands that affluence needs to find a flexible balance among citizens. Otherwise the body politic becomes dysfunctional because oligarchs are few and the people are many. There are ways to combat inequality while insuring that your network's assets are sufficient to protect it against incursions. Optimizing distribution of wealth is not a mystery, although it is often mystified by oligarchic interests seeking to improve their share. The right balance means sustainable growth. Imbalances incur existential risks for oligarchs; the solution is not greater inequality.

In matters of state and corporate security, police, soldiers, and security personnel are most effective when they are citizens and employees. Mercenaries, temporary workers, and consultants are often useless or dangerous. Although you don't have to manage their benefit packages, such self-determination may be a greater danger than that freedom. If an oligarch controls an organization through the arms, skills, and strategies of mercenaries, temporary workers, and consultants, you will stand neither firm nor safe, since they are disunited, ambitious, greedy, and unfaithful, valiant before friends and cowardly before enemies, and cause serious problems in projects from their lack of commitment.

When a real conflict arises, the lead consultant, who aspires to be an oligarch, will come to you asking what you would like to do now that all is in shambles. When the consultant approaches you in this way, he or she calculates how much more profit there is in your relationship, assessing whether it is possible, based your frustration and fear, to gain full control, whether it's best to cut and run with the profits already billed, and whether to offer consulting services and the knowledge of your systems to your competitors.

Mercenaries and consultants fear neither your authority nor infidelity to their contract. Destruction is deferred only as long as action is deferred. In peace, one is robbed by these contractors, and in war, one is robbed by the enemy. The fact is that they have no other attraction to you or reason for keeping the field or their contract than the trifle of their hourly wages, which is not sufficient to make them willing to die for you or even assign their best personnel, but rather charge you full price for a herd of newly minted MBAs or soldiers cashiered out of the regulars for brutality. They are ready enough to be your soldiers and consultants while you do not make war or are in the planning stages, but when war or the real work of a project begins, they will take themselves off the job and bring in independent consultants at a hefty premium, or run from the foe. If they do not run, you are in worse luck, because to protect themselves they will be excessively violent. A deeper problem than losing any battle develops from mercenaries skilled in torture and high-handed treatment of indigenous citizens.

Obamacare was delayed, Obama's regime jeopardized, and people suffered without health insurance because of his consultants and the faith he placed in them. The ruin of Iraq and one of the chief failures of US action in that benighted country was caused by nothing else than resting hopes on mercenaries first for fighting and then for training. The Iraqi army and Shia militia avoided battle because their officers were corrupt and instilled no loyalty in the troops; no amount of training can change an officer's corruption. The Kurds, on the other hand, fight in hope of a nation of their own. They are loyal, fearless, and honorable on the field of battle. Yet the US military continues to hire mercenaries because of their management's political connections and the officers' fear that young soldiers will be killed through their mismanagement, and that the resulting bad press will weaken the nation's resolve.

Some mercenaries and consultants, of course, are highly skilled. So, if the task is specific enough, they can be cost effective. Still, in the long run, the oligarch must provide benefits and stability to workers and soldiers who are devoted to the firm and the country. Hence, working with your own people brings long-lasting rewards.

The reason mercenaries and consultants appear useful is excessive financialization of corporate and government activities and failure to look at the entire ecosystem of a business or nation. In financial companies, the same problem occurs because similar conditions exist at different scales. During the Industrial Revolution in Europe and the US, assets were accumulated by oligarchs and their workers as never before in history. But from 1914 through 1970, the greatest destruction of assets in the history of humanity took place through two world wars, the Great Depression, the revolutions of Russia and China, and the Korean and Viet Nam wars. Destruction was caused by the failure of oligarchs, in all parts of the globe, to understand their collective responsibility.

Instead, competition for colonies, rather than mutual aid and support of populations, was a core policy in Europe from the Austro-Hungarian Empire to the German industrialists prior to WWII to the European plundering of China. Winner-take-all competition was also a key motivation for individuals in global equity and debt markets. The system of imperial accumulation and oligarchic inequality peaked in the years before WWI resulting in general chaos and the breakdown of alliances, due to concentrations of wealth that made many oligarchs think themselves independent of the network that sustained them.

The conceptual failure that links competition to individual well-being, impairing balance in many societies, continues to this day. The US, EU, China, Russia, India, and their local business ventures are being plundered today, not by invading hordes or traitorous mercenaries, but by corporate oligarchs—arms and pharmaceutical manufacturers, the financial industry, industrial agriculture, mining interests that are oblivious to the ecosystems they dig in, and transportation that ignores its impact on the atmosphere, as well as various neoliberal globalists and libertarians—who misunderstand themselves, their organizations, and their mutual dependencies. These individuals and small groups fall prey to delusions of freedom stimulated by instantaneous communication and the illusions of marketing. They fail to see that the wealth of nations and of oligarchs comes from integrated action among all parts of society, not from profiteering by any one sector or individual.

Today, such destruction of assets threatens to occur again from income inequality that has become so great that, as of 2014, the top 1 percent in the US owns 47 percent of all assets and the top 0.1 percent owns 15.5 percent, with differences among classes continuing to increase. These ratios are unsustainable because they require the rich to support society. But there are too few rich people to buy enough goods to keep factories humming and stores stocked. The workers and middle classes, which are the engines of growth and prosperity in post-industrial developed societies, are being legislated out of their wages and pensions. These large middle classes don't have sufficient regular income, due to globalization's deflation and surplus labor, to buy enough goods and services, or for corporations and governments to support their ecosystems. An improved ratio of wealth distribution that wise oligarchs can coordinate, if they realize its importance before society collapses again, maintains power longer. The rich become richer, while the middle class and the poor have enough to sustain demand.

As of 2015, Mario Draghi (an ex-Goldman Sachs employee) planned $75Bn/month in a quantitative easing program for the European Central Bank. The Bank of England, with another ex-Goldman employee in charge, announced the continuation of their $35Bn/month Quantitative Easing program. Japan continued their $80Bn/month QE program, and the US Federal Reserve Bank was still buying $80Bn/month of treasuries, with the People's Republic Bank of China probably buying a similar amount. That's $350Bn/month or $4.2 trillion per year being pumped into the global

CHAPTER XII: HOW MANY KINDS OF ASSETS, WORKERS, AND SOLDIERY... 65

economy by central banks in support of the banking system. These purchases cause financial repression, hurting savers—the poor who hope to save enough to be able to afford a home and the elderly who hope to save enough money for rent and necessities once they can no longer work. The money from central banks isn't being invested in jobs and infrastructure for those who support the economy with their labor and spending. These gains are book entries to governments and banks and socked away by corporate leaders taking oversized bonuses. There is little trickle down despite the ubiquity of that phrase, since there's a limit to the number of antique cars, vintage wines, and impressionist paintings that oligarchs can buy and sell to each other. Politically, the number of global conflicts grows as inequality and climate change degrade societies both physically and through fear of change.

To demonstrate further the inappropriateness of these financial and military arrangements, we can say that financial and armaments corporations, if not led by capable men, make serious mistakes. If these leaders are skillful, other oligarchs must be cautious, because, in the current culture of leadership, they work primarily for their own gain, either by oppressing other leaders or their workers and soldiers. These financial and armaments leaders are not to be trusted, since the ideology of most corporate management today does not acknowledge that oligarchs are dependent on the societies that spawned their wealth. Instead, financial, military, and other executives seek to subvert laws and regulation for short-term benefit and profit in financial markets, but most of all to keep their jobs.

Contemporary corporate culture makes it seem that achievement relies solely on individual skills, which we have seen is insufficient for broad progress or prosperity. On the other hand, if the industrial captain is not skillful in subverting laws and regulations, the society is ruined in the usual way, by the collapse of vital institutions and financial instability. Only by systematically engaging individual skills through a network of like-minded individuals, who support a well-regulated society with well-maintained infrastructure, can general well-being be secured, progress be encouraged, and wealth managed sustainably over years and generations, which are after all the goals of civilization.

One might be tempted to suggest that leaders act the same way—for the benefit of the institution, its people, and themselves—whether or not they have skin in the game. However, a financial manager paid by the quality of deals rather than their number will more likely support institutional and social ecosystems. Reflect on what motivates you. When arms and wealth must be used, then an oligarch, as one of the duties of leadership, should invest with some of your own assets if you expect to profit directly. You cannot always judge how much pressure you have to apply to a situation in advance, so flexibility and good fortune play as important a role as ethics. Simple judgements are rarely adequate to complex situations, although in the end an oligarch must be decisive or risk being overcome by events.

Oligarchs benefit by supporting citizens and workers with managers who have the interests of the networks in mind as much as their own profit. When a manager is worthy, leadership should use contracts, rewards, and cajolery to keep that manager in place until major projects are completed and suitable replacements found. Manager's salaries should be kept within reasonable bounds, but always high enough that their interests align with yours and not with workers. If the manager fails, he or she must be removed.

If leaders switch in and out of office whenever it's convenient, the stockholders and citizens become rightly suspicious of their motives. In Argentina, for example, presidents swap in and out of office whenever self-dealing administration policies bankrupt the nation. Then similar policies are implemented by the next administration. Companies owned by remote oligarchs are in a similar situation to the one we discussed with Deutsche Bank and its US subsidiary. Trump's use of family to manage his assets during his presidency can only be interpreted as using state office to line his own pockets. Naked self-dealing should where possible be avoided as resentment will always make such an administration short-lived rather than dynastic. The failure of others in Trump's party to object to his using public office for private gain can only be interpreted as an indication of their own desire to freeload upon the societies they serve in the same way.

An oligarch benefits from paying attention to the inevitable results of inequality and poorly motivated participants. In the current climate of unfettered accumulation, an oligarch's intentions are best disguised to grow assets sustainably. Otherwise, the political leader or corporate manager will be understood by the people to be simply another part of the power-hungry crowd. After a while, the people will always look to change that transparently self-serving leadership, since they are not participating as well. It is common wisdom that an oligarch must avoid expanding in the wrong way. Yet many oligarchs today aren't sufficiently careful to grow organically, because organic growth is less profitable. They are chary of growing by prudent acquisition because such return on investment may not garner enough headlines. Growth by acquisition may be used effectively, when the cost of entry is otherwise too high, and then only in line with a well-understood business model consistent with the organization's culture.

Daimler-Benz's purchase of Chrysler for $36 billion in 1998 is an example of a poorly executed acquisition. Ultimately, Chrysler's focus on accommodating car buyers with lower incomes did not fit with Daimler-Benz's luxury car business model. Therefore, in 2007, Daimler-Benz had to pay $650 million to Cerberus Capital Management to sever its ties with Chrysler.

This famed "merger of equals" did little to support Chrysler's underdog strategy that had reduced its product development costs to 2.8 percent of revenues, half that of other major car companies. By subordinating the once entrepreneurial Chrysler to the top-down management style of Daimler-Benz, the workers of Chrysler became disheartened, management costs spiraled out of control, and the "cowboy culture" of Chrysler that was in reality driven by workers at all levels, appropriately motivated to perform, could not function under the German managers.

In fact, this "merger of equals" was always intended to subordinate Chrysler, contrary to the advertised purpose. The merger damaged Chrysler's brand. The American dynamism faded under German pressure, and the Germans failed to engage their managers productively.

The removal of four or five key leaders from Chrysler's management team had doomed the merger. Chrysler CEO Bob Eaton had appeared withdrawn from and became dispassionate about the company he continued to run. Even Daimler's CEO Jürgen Schrempp encouraged Eaton to "act like a co-chairman and step up to the podium...," but to no avail. Two valuable vice presidents, engineer Chris Theodore and manufacturing specialist Shamel Rushwin, left for jobs at Ford. According to then-President Peter Stallkamp, Eaton "had really checked out about a year before he left." The other managers feared for their careers, and in the absence of assurance, they assumed the worst. Workers who feel disenfranchised tend to be disaffected rather than invested in their jobs. Disgruntled workers drive employers to automate which only makes the job situation direr.

Of all the different kinds of soldiers, executives, consultants, and politicians, the most helpful to an oligarch are those aligned with the culture of the state or company. Outsiders may be useful in the short term to shake up an entropic organization, but unless a thorough cultural realignment is planned, as when Woodrow Wilson planned with Edward Bernays to change how Europe viewed the United States, leaders in any oligarchic network should seek to align similar components. Divergence, on the other hand, is the primary mechanism of change for individuals, groups, and ecosystems.

Chapter XIII: Concerning Auxiliaries or Foreign Troops and Assets, and One's Own

Foreign assets and troops are often employed when national resources are stretched thin. Iraqi Shia leaders employed both US and Iranian forces in their fight against Islamic State and Sunni insurgents. These foreign arms and assets may have been expedient, but they can be disadvantageous for the oligarch who uses them. If foreigners end up controlling land or other holdings, such as oil profits, those assets are lost or, worse, they may destabilize an entire domain.

If a war is lost, foreign fighters simply go home as the South Vietnamese discovered. Winning, foreigners capture local assets. The Iraqis might have learned about foreign troops during the second Gulf War. Now, with both Iranian, US, and even Russian troops fighting in the region, there is little hope for the Shia of Iraq to control their own fate. They will become a client state of Iran or fall further into the clutches of US oil companies, and their people will be further oppressed.

At the end of the Cold War, the Chinese economy initially benefited from investments by newly empowered Western globalists. However, Chinese leadership soon realized that relying on Western investment to bolster their economic development was not a successful long-term strategy. They have now taken their gains from the West and begun to develop a consumer society where wealth is generated from a more robust internally driven process. But it will take a long time to build a consumer society, including the re-education of a culture habituated to saving rather than consuming. Also, having gained from foreign investment, Chinese globalists are loath to relinquish control. So even in the well-regulated, top-down Chinese state, internecine struggles have forced Xi Jinping to begin an anticorruption campaign to sever globalist cash flows and claw back some of the assets blocking internalization.

An oligarch who has no desire to conquer or expand can make use of foreign arms and assets, for they prevent growth while appearing to save the day. They are more hazardous than mercenaries or debt because with them your ruin is readymade. Foreign assets and soldiers primarily support their own oligarchs no matter how you position or postpone reckoning. Among mercenaries, deceit is most dangerous; with foreigners, valor. Savvy oligarchs, therefore, have always avoided these foreign arms and assets except when they wish to pillage their own country. The one exception is the use of foreign asset sales by financial leaders at the end of a business cycle. Many of those assets sold to foreigners can then be repurchased later at lower prices.

Aggressive oligarchs, willing to take risks, attempt to build markets in traditional cultures to buy their natural resources and cheap manufactures for resale while selling mining equipment and Coca-Cola back to their markets. Yet many of these traditional cultures resist the intrusions of US companies, remembering how colonial empires threatened or destroyed their societies. The US was not only thwarted in Cuba and Iran, but wherever a war appears, the wise oligarch can look for a failed commercial negotiation and subsequent conflict with indigenous oligarchs. Whether Viet Nam in the '60s, the former Yugoslavia in the '90s, or the Middle East today, US corporations attempted to inject their assets into foreign economies to stimulate local demand for US goods and services and to buy local assets cheaply. The failure to do so successfully can only be blamed on the inability of corporate leaders and policymakers to understand that others' cultures may act differently, or that they were simply seeking a deal in which only one side really benefited. Most oligarchs, whether from Cleveland or Calcutta, want to negotiate a good deal and to benefit their society. Very few are willing to gain at the expense of their own people, although some ruling oligarchies have such one-sided cultures.

US oligarchs market a message of freedom. They have convinced their own people that they are free and assumed that other cultures will believe that, too. Realistically, this freedom can now be best understood as freedom for oligarchs, from the Founding Fathers to Sam Walton, to strip value from citizens and use it for personal gain. Thus, society deteriorates and inequality grows. The notion that leadership improves the people's situation appears to have been lost. Contemporary oligarchs can rectify this situation by improving the well-being of the citizens and workers.

Some foreign oligarchs enter into contracts with US oligarchs that look good at first, but which hide an indigenous toxin. That poison, oddly, turns out to be an excess of the self-determination, independence, and freedom that the corporate media has convinced US citizens are theirs by birth and by the Constitution. This narrow idea of freedom ignores the fact that individuals do not thrive alone, but need others and connections to them that build wealth and secure surplus for future use. If oligarchs cannot understand the will of others until it is too late, they are not leaders, but only avaricious and short sighted. This insight is often lost in the heady rush of ambition.

The British empire operated in a similar way. Merchants bought natural resources and luxury goods in Asia, Africa, and the Americas and resold them in England. British merchants with foreign office support cut favorable deals with local leaders, establishing a network for trade and a global supply chain. These asset flows sometimes operated in competition with industrial production in Britain. For example, British merchant ships, loaded with bullion, purchased spices, tea, and textiles from Asia. The textiles, however, created competition with British textile manufacturing oligarchs who producing similar industrial goods in Britain. To save local industry, the British government in support of its industrialists undermined the Indian textile industry to create a market for textiles from Lancashire. In the longer term, however, the British became too dependent on foreign markets and could not adapt to new conditions.

Sometimes the merchants could not secure markets through the soft power of trade. Then the government and the Hudson's Bay Company or the British East India Company, whose directors were from the same network of public school as the government representatives, were forced to colonize. Colonization cost British taxpayers a pretty penny, but enriched the trading companies. Here we see how historical cash flows, associated with public/private partnerships, and tax dollars are used to create markets overseas. The details of British Empire balance sheets require many volumes of their own to discuss.

We do not wish to leave this topic without addressing recent instances of multinational corporations using overseas workers to lower the wages paid to North American and European workers. Free-trade agreements, initiated by developed states, create an oversupply of workers globally that lowers the cost of labor, consistent with the law of supply and demand. Meanwhile workers in developed nations continued to be pressured to consume through advertising and false promises about economic growth. Thus, the US and EU, because of low wages, fell into a deflationary cycle, which is more dangerous to the oligarchy than higher wages, since it creates conflict between oligarchs and resistance from the people. The short-term gains of global oligarchs empowered developing nations and nationalists in developed countries. Will these globalists be able recover their control of capital flows, labor, and other assets? Is globalization irrevocable or will local cultures reassert themselves as we discussed earlier with religion?

Seeking excessive profit for a few at the expense of citizens and workers does not benefit oligarchs long term. This is especially true in democracies, as oligarchs are discovering. In these days of slow growth, globalists are losing control of their organizations to nationalists who promise renewed prosperity for workers. But those proclaiming the virtue of small government have also overplayed their hand in regimes that they already largely control. The farsighted oligarch realizes that state-sponsored redistribution of wealth will now be a boon for corporations and workers alike. Taking more from the middle and lower classes has little additional upside even for the top 0.1 percent.

With legislatures worldwide promoting fiscal austerity in an effort to lower the cost of government, central banks can only slightly improve the economic balance as we saw throughout the Obama administration. Without fiscal stimulus, monetary stimulus can only be marginally effective after the first few quarters. Forcing economies into further financialization and stagnation, low interest rates and low government spending fails to build assets and jobs. It exacerbates income inequality and seems to have had little impact on deflation. It is unclear whether spending on infrastructure, as proposed by the Trump administration, can reverse this downward spiral. So far, conservatives have been unwilling to fund infrastructure spending through taxation, since the US Congress and also the UK and EU parliaments stick to their low spending rhetoric.

US-based oligarchs have enriched themselves at the expense of their own future and the future of their country, and have compromised the global economic ecosystem. This strategy also puts leadership at risk of social unrest from nationalist conservatives, as we see in the rise of politicians like Trump, the Brexit group, and right-wing parties in Europe. The conservatives' position that economic failure has been the fault of government, not business excesses, misses the point that these fiscal conservatives have been in control for years, making governments increasingly ineffective. Globalists may spin this to their advantage, if conservatives do not first create a widespread war and climate catastrophe with its concomitant problems. But at this point, globalist corporations have aligned with nationalist conservatives to keep low-tax, low-regulation, low-wage strategies in place throughout the developed world. Their short-term gains, like those of the British Empire, will have a destructive long-term effect on global networks.

Income inequality, when it reaches certain levels, promotes social unrest as it did in 1914 and 1789. Deflation in the EU has been even worse than in the US, with negative interest rates in many of the EU countries in 2015–17. Europe is also threatened by incursions from hostile Islamic forces, immigration caused by drought and war in the Middle East, and self-aggrandizing Russian forces in the Ukraine and Belarus. The EU has begun to fail with the collapse of the Greek economy and Italian banks, as well as the UK vote to exit the EU. War is already beginning to spread and will only worsen if oligarchs continue to take more of the pie than their societies can tolerate.

We conclude that no oligarchy is secure without having an appropriate balance between its own assets and a network of acknowledged dependencies. A culture that recognizes leadership's responsibility for the whole of society appears as such a protective strategy and long precedes human society. A large tree shelters many other life forms. It inhibits the growth of smaller trees, but does not kill them. It uses the diversity of species under its canopy, from plants to microbes, to support its growth. This description is not a metaphor, but rather a biological similarity between human and non-human organizations.

Human leaders, to build support and secure their own position, must understand clearly how the needs and skills of those they shelter improve their own condition. The forces and assets they use to defend themselves and the stability of their network depend on maintaining social contracts. A good contract benefits both parties and is not a zero-sum, winner-take-all deal. Excessive reliance on assets and arms of others make an oligarch dependent on good fortune, not having the skills that in adversity would defend you. Nothing can be so uncertain or unstable as power founded on the weakness and ignorance of citizens and workers. The greatest forces for the security of the state, the commercial enterprise, and oligarchs themselves are the health, education, and welfare of their citizens and workers. An alliance between workers and leadership benefits both to the greatest extent possible. Human cooperation is our most productive skill: treating every transaction as competitive fails to produce long-term gains and finishes far behind those who work together, as any experienced oligarch knows.

Technology leaders like Gates, Jobs, and Mark Zuckerberg organized their firms around the intelligence of their workers as much as their inventions and investment. Their strategies can be emulated in constructing a mutually supportive society that also builds great wealth for leadership. The ideology of individualism isolated and separated from that of mutual aid may be easily seen as a way to weaken the well-being and will of national institutions, even though such ideas are attractive to an oligarch's self-esteem.

Chapter XIV: That Which Concerns the Oligarch on the Subject of the Art of Finance

An oligarch in the modern world ought to focus on the study of finance—its rules and its discipline. The art of finance, as much as war and digital technology, belongs to those who control the state and the corporation. To acquire control of a nation or company requires financing wars, factories, inventions, and political networks. Even great ideas, if not properly financed, may fail or become subject to hostile takeover, as has so often happened to technology startups. When oligarchs have thought more of the short- than the long-term financially, they have often lost their states, their companies, and their families.

The US, through its well-controlled finances and soldierly behavior in WWI, became the leading country of the world. Woodrow Wilson's government used the conflict to buy war materiel from US manufacturers and turned a recession into a boom. This process seemed to bolster the oligarchy. But since the war cost 50 percent of the nation's gross national product, or GDP, the oligarchs lost more through that war than they gained, seeing short-term advantage but ignoring the longer term. This short-term failure was only the beginning.

As pointed out above and by Thomas Piketty in *Capital in the Twenty-First Century*, by 1970, the gap between asset owners and workers was as small as ever in history. Global communication, ideas, and trade toppled oligarchies throughout the world. The US oligarchs who made those short-term financial decisions in WWI and during the Roaring Twenties had been largely replaced by New Deal Democrats and European social democrats who supported workers more than their predecessors. The attractions of war had turned out badly for most oligarchs. Furthermore, war profiteers get very rich very quickly, and collisions of interest are unavoidable. These conflicts and the clashes between oligarchs that cause wars are the chief threat to the oligarchy and its power, yet many oligarchs remain thrilled by the spice of war.

The rules of oligarchy were not broken by broader democracy or by the social spending of the twentieth century. Rather oligarchy was strengthened by the increased participation of citizens and workers. Representative democracy usually improves well-being for the majority, but oligarchs remain in control of states and corporations in spite of the excitement generated by suffrage and consumerism. And more individuals and intermediate institutions directly contribute to oligarchic control through participation in financial markets, buying goods and services, and voting for leaders at all levels of government.

Rebuilding destroyed infrastructures after WWII allowed workers in corporations and small businesses to create a dynamic global economy. States were encouraged by the chaos of global conflict and the threat of nuclear war to export soft power. They also benefited greatly from reconstructing factories, housing, transport, agriculture, and mining in partnership with corporations. Both the people and leadership benefited. Unfortunately, arms makers overplayed their hand in Viet Nam through an alliance with the security state. Then the counterculture, civil rights movements, and other popular movements threatened conservative corporate leaders who pushed against liberal governance, unleashing the full power of oligarchic protectionism. Since the "Powell Memorandum" of 1971, through fear of losing the ideological reins of politics, corporate leaders in the US, UK, and elsewhere have radically increased their share of the pie by financializing societies around the world. Thus, they subverted the form of democracy.

Recently, however, these globalists became victims of their own ideology and now find it difficult to extricate themselves from a dilemma. Financial arrangements that support the oligarchy—free capital flows with restricted labor flows—require technological change to implement them effectively. Such change is followed in every case by social change that subverts the cultural stability that binds masses of voters to conservatives and populists, demanding more oligarchic connivance than usual.

By successfully infiltrating both the Democratic and Republican parties, conservative oligarchs have managed to maintain control through private foundations, as well as from the 2010 Supreme Court decision in the case of Citizens United v. Federal Elections Commission, and other court decisions. As a result, a US president can be liberal while Congress and the courts are conservative, and the oligarchy profits from both parties. Three-digit ROI accrues from such successful political investment by conservative corporate leaders. Corporations are strengthened as government is weakened, reducing its ability to balance diverse interests. It binds government more closely to business to the short-term benefit of oligarchy. Now Trump's administration seeks to promote a consolidated conservative program that would reverse much of the New Deal and threaten renewed oligarchic conflict as well as conflict with several segments of working and middle-class voters. In the longer term, wise oligarchs support networks that include both the workers and implementers of policy, as in Venice during its heyday and the US during its period of greatest strength just after WWII when workers and corporations all benefited. Mutual support of all classes of society is more sustainable than societies where only a few thrive.

Conservatives, though, are right about one thing. It is only through continuous application of effort that oligarchs maintain their position. Carter, for example, was a key oligarch in government and the Trilateral Commission, but when he left office, his focus on the ethical principles of society pushed him to the margins. On the other hand, Clinton went from oligarchic president to fundraiser for globalization in international finance, lining the pockets of himself and his friends through emerging markets development projects. Clinton continues to share in the spoils, offering improvements in living standards to many poor nations. It is not clear if renewed nationalism in the US and EU will discourage oligarchs in emerging markets from handing over further control to globalists.

Leaders vying for power need a full understanding of finance and clear financial objectives for both the short and long term. Through limited war, financial engineering, and global control of resources, leading oligarchs have now recovered from the folly of twentieth-century warfare, but winner-take-all financial dealings threaten their gains.

So-called Objectivism challenges civil oligarchs by pitting individuals against the group rather than recognizing that individuals and groups are interdependent. This divergent philosophy supports a shift of power visible in the election of Trump, Brexit, and other events. It may already be destabilizing global networks at the very time that climate change requires collective action.

Investment and growth are suppressed when oligarchs rely completely on their own devices to develop their wealth and connections, rather than allowing oligarchic networks and civil order to protect property. While as we have already said, the oligarch must be able to rely on indigenous assets and arms in times of trouble, the social fabric and individual wealth are both strengthened by trade and increasing wages for workers. Thus, the wealth of civil oligarchs generally exceeds that of warlords and single-family oligarchies. Oligarchs protected by civil law become richer and more powerful as the society increases in wealth. They need to spend less of their wealth on defense, since they can rely on taxation of the citizens to pay for most defense and security. Yet these facts seem to be ignored by conservative and libertarian oligarchs pathologically fearful of relinquishing any control to the network of human social structure.

Conservatives, libertarians, and evangelical Christians have been funding their networks for nearly fifty years. Since the peak of economic equality in 1970 and the publication of the Powell Memorandum, many aspects of society that were formerly not considered financial have been financialized. And financialization has even deeper roots. War was historically paid for by rich people, but since the Civil War in the US, when the government sold bonds to 5 percent of the population to fund the war, and then the Franco-Prussian War that solidified the public financing of conflict, war has been increasingly financialized.

Payment for medical care has historically been progressive, but in the absence of single-payer health care in the US, complex financial arrangements dominate medicine and compromise the quality of care through a focus on expensive treatment options and big research projects. Education has turned institutions of higher education into building projects that enrich board members and their developer cronies at the expense of students. Common infrastructure was usually the domain of the state, but theories of small government and failure to find a way for oligarchs to profit from infrastructure projects has made Congress unwilling to pay for maintaining US infrastructure with predictable deterioration. Trump wants to alter this tendency, sadly at the wrong time of the business cycle.

Liquidity is a double-edged sword, deluding wealthy oligarchs worldwide and making oligarchs feel wealthier than they actually are. They feel more successful than competitors who have with fewer liquid assets even with greater wealth. Withdrawal of liquidity makes them feel poorer, so that anxiety about nominal wealth prioritizes speculation over investment. As climate threats increase, financiers focus on hard assets, exposing significant risks to financialization. As a shrewd oligarch, you will not be duped into putting all your eggs in financial baskets. Thus, knowing the limits of finance represents one critical element of good financial knowledge.

As a response to reduced growth in developed economies since 1970 and the postwar rebuilding of Europe and the US being largely completed, governments debased their currencies by creating wealth through debt. Bankers and other purveyors of credit encouraged governments to rely on deficit spending, corporations to borrow huge sums to increase gross holdings, and consumers to buy on credit, even when they didn't have the collateral. Often, the rates charged for that borrowing used to be considered legally usurious, but were justified to legislatures via lobbying pressure from global banking interests and the credit-card industry, to the detriment of the middle class and the debasement of developed-country currencies.

CHAPTER XIV: THAT WHICH CONCERNS THE OLIGARCH ON THE SUBJECT OF... 77

Financing with debased currency incurs the disrespect of developing countries. Even poverty-stricken Islamic states with little credit, like Yemen, see Western weakness. An oligarch ought to guard against such ignominies, because there is nothing proportionate between good financing and speculative risk. Since one sustains and the other causes suspicion, it is not possible for them to work well together or even to be compared. So, the social fabric begins to unravel, not because debt itself is a problem, but because debt should be incurred primarily when acquiring long-term assets, not to fund speculation.

An oligarch who does not understand the art of finance, in addition to the misfortunes already mentioned, is disrespected by venture capital. Venture capitalists, the funders of new technology, will become unreliable, undermining funded projects in the marketplace to hedge the risk of their investments. This is true for both businesses and governments. A leader, therefore, would be advised to keep these details of finance in mind.

When an organization's senior leaders have a strong financial compass, it's easier for them to resist the investment bankers' siren songs of financial engineering, excessive leverage, and the idea, common during boom times, that somehow the established guidelines of economics no longer apply. Misconceptions like these—which can lead oligarchs to make value-destroying decisions and slow down entire economies—take hold with surprising and disturbing ease since all organisms, including humans, seek to thrive, as we have pointed out, with the lowest possible expenditure of energy.

For the oligarch, wealth is a function of returns on capital, land, and other hard assets, as well as growth. The worker, having few assets, only benefits from economic growth. Therefore, it is vital for an oligarch to focus on growth for long-term security and share the fruits proportionately with workers and citizens. Yet even on a planet of Earth's girth, growth cannot be perpetual along one vector. Populations will be contained, either sooner through human governance or later by ecosystem governance.

It doesn't matter how you slice the pie with financial engineering, share repurchases, or acquisitions. Only improving human well-being creates real value for companies and nations. Efficiency alone does not assure the value of labor, which is the other component of production besides assets that the oligarch controls. Farsighted leaders understand that the balance of economies is like balance in the biosphere. If one component becomes too dominant, the whole functions less well. A good example of this problem is the "snowball earth" theory that our planet was frozen pole to pole many hundreds of millions of years ago, when overpopulation of blue-green algae produced too much oxygen. Our production of greenhouse gases may have a similar if opposite effect. While this outcome is not certain, prudent oligarchs benefit by hedging this risk.

Changes in a nation's currency or company's share price reflect changes in expectations about its performance, not just actual performance such as success in war, wealth of citizens, growth, and real returns on invested capital. The higher those expectations, the better that nation or company must perform just to keep up. Expectations have different values to different citizens, owners, and potential owners—a value based on how they manage the nation or the company, and what strategy they pursue. Different expectations create a diversity of views of the social fabric and different interests must be acknowledged or the society unravels. Diversity of interests remains the primary reason that societies need government and corporations need management.

For example, when in the 1970s the United States stopped improving worker's wages relative to the cost of the basic goods and services, the reputation of the country fell. With the collapse of the Soviet Union in 1989, the United States' reputation, after a brief rise, continued to descend, since no class in US stepped up to lead for all. Conservative media continued to attack all government activity and liberal media never understood how to explain the value of governance.

Since value is usually comparative, a corollary to the social contract, the weaknesses and rising inequality of the United States were laid bare without complementary strengths being revealed. Both the illusion of freedom and, in fact, citizens' actual freedoms decreased. Private and inherited wealth, China, fundamentalist Islam, financial city-states like Singapore, and global corporations all stepped in to fill the vacuum. Without social cohesion or any reason to think of the nation as a unit, the great wealth of the US has been funneled into the pockets of individuals.

Ignoring both principles of finance and the limits of finance leads to poor decisions that erode the value of countries and companies. Consider what happened during the run-up to the recession that began in 2007. Participants in the securitized-mortgage market all proposed that securitizing uncollateralized mortgages reduced the risk of the subprime assets. But the initial risks of each mortgage remained because similar subprime mortgages were simply lumped together without the change in risk profile that would occur if diverse mortgage types were mingled. Securitizing the assets enabled the risks to be passed on to new owners. In this case, the risks and losses were eventually transferred to the public through manipulations by US Treasury officials. These people took public office, but continued to operate in their roles as oligarchs and did not neglect their personal interests and those of their class. Sheila Bair at the Federal Deposit Insurance Corporation was a rare exception to self-dealing governance in the Bush administration. This tendency continues to be enhanced by the Trump administration's self-dealing practices.

Obvious as this seems in hindsight, a great many smart people, who disingenuously claim to have missed it at the time, were working fast and furious to transfer losses from their bank's books to the national balance sheet. The same thing happens every day in executive suites and boardrooms as managers and company directors evaluate acquisitions, divestitures, projects, and executive compensation. Executive compensation has built for the first time a class of workers whose wealth grows at the same pace as growth of assets (4–5 percent). Executive compensation at this level insures that the interests of management are not related to worker compensation or to the value of the company, but to the growth of assets. Compensation at these levels allies managers' interests with those of the asset holders, rather than workers insuring that investors' interests stay paramount. Moreover, even the interests of companies are often ignored in order to secure the interests of management, so they can keep their jobs. When such individuals begin to work in government, they often pursue those same private interests as much as they can, so government appears problematic when it's actually the failure of these new officials to support the interests of the country they serve.

Finally, and on the other side of the coin, financialization can easily be mistaken for knowledge of the country or the company's business. While financial knowledge remains one of the keys to oligarchic power, finance can only be understood properly by knowing its place among non-financial activities. Those who work in the oligarchy as servants of wealth, such as the accountants and lawyers of the income defense industry and intellectuals in many disciplines, inappropriately justify financialization. Oligarchy cannot be simply a set of individuals of wealth as economic determinists claim. The true power of oligarchy lies as already pointed out in the networks and connections that transfer control from person to person and between organizations for the purpose of maintaining power, examples of influence by very wealthy individuals notwithstanding.

For if we separate wealth alone, we lose sight of the fact that highly productive individuals tend to seek out others who achieve great things. If an oligarch is focused solely on financialization, the surrounding country or company may be ignored. The oligarch is then less able to undertake its support and defense. If failing to understand the major contributions made to the state and to the corporation by those who do not accumulate wealth, organizations flounder due to lack of support by the people—citizens and workers. By knowing and observing your locality, by understanding the impact of your actions on surroundings, as an oligarch, you more readily recognize any related subject that needs analysis, understanding, and action. This is true because the ups and downs, stability, and new technologies resemble each other, forming similar shapes at different scales. Even changes in climate that are part of any ecosystem or changes among individuals, corporations, states, or planets resemble each other as much or more than they are dissimilar. These similarities help an effective oligarch decide how power, growth, and opportunity may be leveraged both for your own benefit and, not coincidentally, for the benefit of the majority.

By understanding the operations of one kind of organization, the observant oligarch often arrives at understanding of others. But all things not being equal, although they are similar, such a broad transfer of knowledge between disciplines, as with the present text, can be deceptive. My knowledge of finance, literature, and ecology do not insure my understanding of sports, manufacturing, agriculture, physics, and other disciplines. Yet epistemologies that are similar throughout the structures of knowledge extend to the biology of each organism.

Disciplinary, bodily, and organizational boundaries and borders are all penetrated by connectors to other disciplines, bodies, organizations, and actions. These are not firm boundaries at all like a wall, but are instead semipermeable membranes. The property metaphor, being two-dimensional, prevents understanding how such domains work. The oligarch who lacks the ability to distinguish the similar from the diverse lacks an essential skill as vital as finance. Such awareness of taxonomy across disciplinary, corporate, and individual boundaries teaches a perspicacious oligarch how to surprise competitors, to select new lines of business that capture the public imagination, to lead initiatives with a minimum of faltering, and to arrange resources to the advantage of your network and other dependencies.

5: Guidance on Oligarchic Comportment

CHAPTER XV: CONCERNING THINGS FOR WHICH ALL PEOPLE, AND ESPECIALLY OLIGARCHS, ARE PRAISED OR BLAMED

What ought to be the rules of conduct for an oligarch towards citizens, employees, and peers? Since many have written on this point, you may consider it presumptuous to mention it again, especially because we are taking a different point of view than the authorities. Nevertheless, to write something useful for you who wish to understand and not simply confirm what you already believe, it appears more appropriate to identify the complexity of these matters than to decorate a generality that stirs our emotions.

Many have idealized the form of government—Aristotle, Hobbes, Jefferson, Marx, Chomsky—describing republics and principalities that never existed. Many have tried to establish a single set of principles for right action. But because humanity cannot be fully represented alone and separate from the rest of the planet, these writer's prior principles remain divorced from the detailed interactions that take place between the layers of political, ethical, and environmental conditions daily played out on many stages. Prioritizing any one discipline, like economics, ethics, and self-interest, under all conditions, however reassuring, cannot be the basis of an oligarch's policies. What's good for the goose is sometimes not good for the glance.

The thorough application of any single principle sooner results in an oligarch's ruin than your preservation. If you wish to live up to your public professions of virtue, you must recognize that important actions often have some elements of uprightness and some of injustice. The oligarch benefits from separating, for example, investments for social utility and investments for personal profit. Mixing these two, while profitable in the short term, leaves a bitter taste in the mouths of your citizens and workers. It sets a bad example for the public and for other leaders. Focusing solely on the idea of your freedom, without understanding how the exercise of freedom, may turn out to be no more than license. And if you ignore fairness and equality, or at least the appearance of them, you expose your regime to internal dissent. An oligarch's fortunes and humanity are reinforced by recognizing the multiple, often contradictory, effects of your actions.

Both oligarchs and planners in oligarchic networks must know how to apply the principles outlined above to balance the multiple effects of their actions and to use them to retain and improve their position. Putting on one side the myths concerning oligarchy, like conspiracy theories, and discussing on the other those acts which are material, all people exhibit qualities which bring them both blame and praise. One is reputed liberal, others miserly. One is reputed generous, one rapacious; one cruel, one compassionate; one faithless, another faithful; one cowardly, another bold and brave; one affable, another arrogant; one lascivious, another chaste; one sincere, another cunning; one hard, another easy; one grave, another frivolous; one religious, another unbelieving; one racist, another less prejudiced; and the like. These characteristics follow the oligarch around, and the media tend to report news items that reinforce these binaries in order to sell papers and capture eyeballs.

Everyone wishes an oligarch to exhibit only the good qualities named above. Such consistent behavior isn't always possible in the public arena or in private business. Because an oligarch's motives and thoughts can't be traced through every complex transaction, it is only necessary to be sufficiently careful to avoid those vices which would lose you your position.

In the run-up to the 2016 US presidential election, FBI Director James Comey acted in a way that both affected the outcome of the election and remains opaque regarding his intention. Within a few days of exonerating Hillary Clinton of any legal wrongdoing with respect to her use of a private email account as secretary of state, Comey announced that the FBI had new information and might open a new inquiry concerning Clinton's emails. His action was significant in changing public opinion regarding Clinton's candidacy. Then once Trump had, with Comey's assistance, won the presidency, Comey refuted Trump's claim that prior President Obama had tapped his phones and began an investigation into Trump's ties with

CHAPTER XV: CONCERNING THINGS FOR WHICH ALL PEOPLE, AND... 83

Russia. Trump's response was to fire Comey, claiming he did so because of Comey's self-serving behavior in speaking about Hillary Clintons emails, but Comey had stopped publicly discussing ongoing FBI investigations of Trump's business dealings, Russian influence, and cases against Trump for sexual misconduct.

It's easy to say that Comey was simply doing his job, serving the cause of justice and upholding the reputation of the FBI for unimpeachable honesty. It is also, however, relevant to say that he created a definitive power base for himself, announcing quite publicly that no one could gain or keep high office without including him and his bureau in the inner circle of decision-making. Hence, the details of such transactions are often opaque or ambiguous. To understand power, therefore, we must look at the outcomes of events to determine their significance and not waste time with unstated motives, praise, and blame because analysis of political systems is not a court of law, but only a way to clarify the ecology of events.

An oligarch should, when possible, avoid those associates who would hurt your reputation. But since, too, this is not always possible, you can employ problematic associates when appropriate, and use public relations to manage opinion with a combination of public press and social media. Colonial powers like the UK and US often find local tyrants like Hosni Mubarak and Saddam Hussein useful in managing their foreign holdings. You don't need to make yourself uncomfortable by incurring blame for those vices without which the state and corporation could only be saved with difficulty. An occasional foray into the territory of a weaker state may do more to improve your popularity with the voters than it hurts you for appearing to bully weaker nations. Neither Reagan's attack on Granada nor Il Duce's on Ethiopia reduced their effectiveness as leaders. For, if considered carefully, something that looks like virtue, if followed, would be ruinous, while something else, which looks like vice, brings you security and prosperity.

An experienced oligarch knows what will bring you praise and blame as well as what blame will hobble your ability to act in the future. As mentioned, political and corporate management focus on outcomes more than ethics. This is not to say that the ends justify the means, but rather that intention doesn't always produce predictable results. Futilely searching for primary cause or ethical intention in complex situations is often nothing more than validating the searcher's self-image.

While trust remains a key component in the success of any activity, it is important to understand that associates can be trusted in some matters but not in others. Not coincidentally, contemporary medical best practices also focus on outcomes as a way to keep costs low and patients healthy over the entire system of medical care. Excellence in caring for the sick includes both quality services and assurance of good outcomes. In other multidisciplinary activities like war and electoral politics, individual actions can only be counted successful if outcomes also are successful. Both short- and long-term results must be documented in order to assess outcomes and which tactics that appear risky may often save the day. An oligarch is better served by attending to the longer term, as long as short-term reversals do not disrupt networks and risk losing one's position. Sometimes, however, you must be willing to lose a battle if the battle is only a distraction in the larger scheme of the war. Strategic sacrifice helps insure longer term goals.

This point certainly does not suggest ignoring the details of transactions. In contemporary electoral politics, focusing on each vote and each category of votes in all jurisdictions determines how oligarchs are viewed by citizens and importantly whether they will win an election. Suppressing the votes of blacks, Hispanics, the elderly, the poor, and students in as many strategic jurisdictions in the US as possible determined Republican control of Congress in 2014 and Trump's victory in the presidential election of 2016 even though he received a minority of votes.

The US Constitution, through the Electoral College, is structured to balance the interests of the states with those of the nation. With increasingly large populations in only a few states, the less populated states have more control than a purer democracy would predict. Thus, practical electoral politics in the US and in other federal systems are successful when controlled by a few local oligarchs who are focused on the operations required to get friendly voters to the polls while suppressing opposition voters rather than focusing on the form of democracy. Electoral practices—purging voter rolls, caging votes by not forwarding registration forms to new addresses, spoiling votes as in the decision on hanging chads in Florida in 2000, blocking people from voting, stuffing ballot boxes, and crosschecking and then purging similar names suppressed in other states—are practical ways of reducing the other party's votes without much chance of being exposed in the media, except in the most superficial way.

Media in the US have little interest in actively questioning the electoral process, even when political parties engage in illegal practices. Media outlets would prefer to provide balanced reporting that avoids incurring the wrath of either side of a dispute and to establish false equivalences that make it difficult to assign blame to either side. Since Karl Rove and other electoral specialists have determined how to control voting out of the public eye, democracy as a form of government appears increasingly ineffective. This weakening of democratic franchise hastens the fall of US power around the globe. Tactical operations establish the order of oligarchy even as an oligarch is advised to maintain a longer view.

Oligarchs are vulnerable when they make complex decisions in the public view. Concern for sustainability and the common good are better drivers of action than morals. Although morals cannot lead oligarchic decisions, public outrage can imperil an office, and the pangs of conscience drain your resolve. Ethical evaluations, framed in a utilitarian manner as fulfilling the potential of a given situation while causing the least harm, may cause bad press and need spinning for different audiences such as Twitter and *Foreign Affairs* magazine. And sometimes such utility spirals out of control in public fora. Hence, balancing contradictory forces and opinions remains the most important skill in governing yourself and others. If your individual capacity for balance fails, you will be brought down by your enemies, although usually, as we have noted, it takes more than one fault to destroy a strong oligarch well positioned in the network.

Chapter XVI: Concerning Liberality and Parsimony

This binary is helpful when analyzing particular strategies and projects. Its value depends more on situations than ethics. When saying that an oligarch is liberal with assets, we are inevitably speaking about specific conditions and events more than personal characteristics. Although personalities may incline one way, the only flaw in an individual would be to try to always be that way.

Remaining cautious about the glitter of dichotomies, we begin with the first of the above-named characteristics. It is useful to be considered liberal, since a tight-fisted oligarch carries the cultural baggage of aristocrats denying peasants a crust of bread and landlords tying virgins to the train tracks. Nevertheless, liberality exercised without bringing you a reputation for it, injures you. For if you exercise liberality honestly, as it should ethically be exercised, it may not become known, and you will not avoid the rebuke of its opposite. Therefore, hoping to maintain a reputation as liberal or at least generous, you are obliged to avoid no expenditure. Acting in this way will soon consume all your property and compel you in the end, if desiring to maintain the label of liberal, to weigh down your citizens with taxes, underpay your employees, and take inappropriate risks to profit.

Such behavior, designed to maintain your liberal reputation, will soon make you odious to your employees and voters. Becoming poor, you will be of little use to anyone. With liberality, having offended many and rewarded few, any financial difficulty jeopardizes your reputation, and the first danger imperils your position. Recognizing these circumstances, and seeking to avoid them, you will tend to reverse your behavior and become miserly.

Frugality is a convenient trait and acts as an appropriate hedge for general governance, an oligarch's long-term plan, and any other class or individual during periods of economic growth. In time, you will be appreciated more for your frugality than for your liberality, since economizing keeps revenues sufficient and state coffers full. You can defend yourself against attacks and engage in enterprises without burdening your citizens, lowering wages, and taking too many risks in the markets and geopolitically. In this way, you exercise liberality toward the masses, who are many, and meanness only toward a few who usually will understand the dynamics of your policies.

Few indeed understand when to apply this rule and when to impress with lavish display, since we have not seen many wonders in historical time except from those who have been considered liberal. The rest, like Bush's tax cuts for bankers and Trump's shocking diplomacy, fail miserably. The reason is that today, as opposed to Machiavelli's day, when the masses had little clout, individuals have far more power, even in totalitarian states, and demand far more from the rich and powerful.

Richard Branson, surely one of Britain's eminent oligarchs, said, "Everything that's really worthwhile in life usually involves some degree of risk and in all we do at Virgin we have always reveled in taking on the seemingly impossible rather than shying away and playing it safe." What can we say to him? Even in Machiavelli's day when the middle class was just emerging, support for the arts—marble statues, grand parades, and magnificent architecture—enhanced the reputations of those we revere today. The Medici and the Doges of Venice all were quite careful how they increased their reputations with art and architectural projects. Even so, both occasionally ran aground their ships of state with excessive spending on grand projects.

An oligarch should not rob workers and investors as corporations like Enron have done, or states, such as Wisconsin under Governor Scott Walker, who removed the right of collective bargaining from public employees, still seek to do. Thievery is not conservative. Rather you should protect your assets, prevent participants in your business and in your

CHAPTER XVI: CONCERNING LIBERALITY AND PARSIMONY 87

political organization from becoming poor and abject so that they are not forced to turn greedy. You ought to generally avoid and at the same time barely pay attention to a reputation for being conservative. For thrift is one of those characteristics which will enable you to lead and your network to benefit from effective communication, offering wage increases and pensions for a secure retirement. Military and financial security for the corporation and the commonweal are key conservative values, although individual greed can be misinterpreted as conservative when it is actually only self-serving in the short term.

Caesar obtained an empire by liberality, and many others have reached the highest rank by broadmindedness and by being so considered. To spend freely either you are a leader in fact, or on your way to become one. In the first case, your liberality is dangerous unless returns on spending, such as donations to political campaigns which as pointed out have a high ROI, promise greater wealth than taking no risk. Also, it is more beneficial to be considered liberal than to actually spend. Caesar wished to become pre-eminent in Rome, but if he had survived, and had not moderated his expenses, he would have destroyed his government, because he was no longer reaping vast fortunes from his conquests as a general. So as in all virtues a conditional and balanced approach makes more sense than believing that all people should behave one way or the other.

Many have been oligarchs and done great things with armies and public works, and they have been considered liberal. But you either spend your own, your employees', and your citizens' wealth, or you spend that of others, or you spend both. In the first case, you ought to be frugal, since others depend on you. In the second, you ought to take any opportunity for liberality, for your expenditures will be managed by the prudent lender, since it is far better to invest the money of others in risky ventures even as it remains important to be seen to put your own skin in the game to gain the trust of your partners. And the third is likely to get you into trouble.

If some leader attacks with an army, supporting it by pillage, sack, and extortion like Al Baghdadi and his cohorts in the Islamic State, stealing that which belongs to others, liberality is required. Otherwise his soldiers would not follow him. Such leaders can readily give what is neither theirs nor their citizens', as did the Saudis and Genghis Khan. Many citizens in developed nations have reached the limits of their patience with moderation and are demanding support from those least willing to actually deliver it, such as Theresa May and Trump. The leaders of developed countries don't pay for the entitlements they give to the people.

Citizens have paid for these benefits with their taxes and their labor with governments only managing them. They are in fact entitled to what they have paid for. Further, government, contrary to the conservative press, manages these large-scale benefits programs far more efficiently than commercial channels like insurance companies that must pay overhead in profits to shareholders and salaries to executives and infrastructure of up to 25 percent. In contrast, governments generally provide benefits at an overhead in the mid-single digits. Any honest conservative will admit these efficiencies. Government overreach does not extend to managing these medical and pension programs. Prudent and thrifty investment of taxes into medical programs and social security measures by leadership in the EU makes the recipients of these social programs loyal, but demanding. Taking away those benefits will alienate people from the state and make even rapacious insurers appear benign.

If the people need pensions and secure retirement, let them pay for it with their taxes, and let government help them secure those assets through social insurance programs like Social Security and nationwide medical systems like those of EU countries or the UK's National Health Service. It is only through a narrow and brittle ideology against government programs that oligarchs, such as Grover Norquist and Charles Koch seek to avoid the small tax of Social Security to help keep the people loyal and productive. The reason for such fragile dogma is that these leaders seek to gain more from direct control of businesses and localities through limited government than they can through national government. Local governments, as already mentioned, are cheaper to control. Lower courts can be readily packed, and management of them is more certain with less financial effort and intellectual energy than controlling a large state or corporation.

Next, you might notice that it does not negatively impact your reputation as much if you waste the assets of others than if you squander your own. There is a problem, however, when you squander the money of others, since you may have difficulty raising funds for your next project. But that is more a matter of your marketing technique than any inherent fallacy associated with invested capital. Many have gone from failure to failure and always raised plenty of money like Bush because he always offered the promise of making more money on the next project. He also had the backing of his network, which remains vast in spite of the financial and foreign policy disarray left by his administration. While his government and the people lost more than a trillion dollars in the Iraq war and more in the financial collapse, through the good offices of Cheney and Hank Paulson, his network made plenty for their investors, so that they supported the war effort and investment banks such as Goldman Sachs through loosening of regulations, helping them avoid prosecution for malfeasance, and providing central bank capital to bolster reserves. Through such examples the importance of operations to the oligarch become manifest, while the form of government is clearly of less influence.

In the intermediate term, there is nothing that wastes as rapidly as liberality when you are in power. While you exercise it, you appear strong and must capitalize on that apparent strength to build a lasting network through sustainable assets. If your power is waning, some short-term gains can be made before you become either poor or despised, or else, by avoiding poverty, you are considered rapacious and hated.

As an oligarch, you should guard, above all things, against being despised and reviled, because those emotions stick in the minds of the people and other oligarchs, and often liberality leads to both. Therefore, it is better for individuals and their networks to have a reputation for frugality and conservatism, which brings reproach in the short term without hatred. Otherwise, seeking a reputation for liberality can incur a name for rapacity which precipitates reproach with hatred as conservatives showed liberals in the 2016 US presidential election.

The intermediate term ethic must be balanced against your long-term legacy which is never lauded unless you are liberal; historians love generosity. Such divergent results that depend on the time frame of your operations are typical of a wise oligarch's planning. Identifying the relevant time frame of any operation is also key in managing ecosystems be they in your corporation or the biosphere.

Chapter XVII: Concerning Cruelty and Clemency, and Whether It Is Better to Be Loved Than Feared

As a leader, you assert qualities that you expect will maintain your position and gain support from your workers and citizens. You always need to convince people that your behavior fits their culture, or you lose adherents. We would like to say that the oligarch ought to desire to be considered kind and not cruel. Nevertheless, you must to take care not to misuse clemency.

As long as oligarchs keep their employees and citizens united and loyal with fair taxes, reliable salaries, and the expectation of a secure retirement, they don't need to worry about the occasional reproach of cruelty.

5: GUIDANCE ON OLIGARCHIC COMPORTMENT

They will, therefore, be more compassionate than those who, through too much mercy, allow disorder to arise from which follows murder and robbery. These crimes injure the entire population, justifying aggressive police tactics in poor neighborhoods that contrast with the lenient treatment of the rich, thus exacerbating resentment among classes.

Efficiency is the defense used to fire workers who wish to organize, while excusing executives conniving in their boardroom to the detriment of the bottom line and support for the society. But those CEOs and police who operate this way often fail to understand how their stability is dependent on the good will of their employees, customers, and citizens.

A new political leader or CEO can hardly avoid a reputation for cruelty or roughness, since new administrations are full of dangers, such as uprooting vested interests, replacing self-serving divisional managers and provincial leaders, and cancelling failing product lines or useless military hardware. Hence Virgil, through the mouth of Dido, excused the inhumanity of her reign because it was new, saying:

> *Res dura, et regni novitas me talia cogunt Moliri, et late fines custode tueri.*
>
> ...against my will, my fate,
> A throne unsettled, and an infant state,
> Bid me defend my realms with all my pow'rs,
> And guard with these severities my shores....

Nevertheless, an oligarch ought, in most cases, be slow to believe and to act. You should not show fear, but proceed in a temperate manner with detailed understanding, prudence, and humanity rather than allow your people to be set against each other. You must consult with others carefully and in private rather than showing too much confidence in public places, thereby appearing immodest. Showing pride in your support of the people and the dignity of your office are notable exceptions. You must be able to trust other leaders or else you will quickly become intolerable. An oligarch should not appear too impetuous or cruel. Otherwise you may lose control of the people as they tend to imitate the behavior of leaders and sports heroes.

Now the question arises whether it is better to be loved than feared. Obviously, one should be able to be either depending on circumstances. Contrary to the usual assumption that it is difficult to unite both attitudes toward one person, any talented politician or corporate leader can appear fearsome to enemies and kind to citizens and employees. But if you have to choose in an ambiguous situation, it is much safer to be feared than loved.

In times of surplus, when economies are growing and crops are plentiful, you can afford to be clement and encourage employees and citizens to love you. Thus, when times are tight or war is at hand, people will understand your cruelties. While you can explain that austerity was required in Greece in 2015 because too many people were employed by the government and the rich were not taxed, other EU countries like Portugal, Italy, and Spain were watching the Greek example thinking of their own debts, and the Germans had apparently forgotten about WWII reparations and how they had been saved from their own foolishness by the Marshall Plan. You protect investments by asking bond holders to take a haircut, taxing everyone to save the state, and firing employees to save the company so that they may be rehired later, perhaps at lower wages.

You may readily assert of people in general that as a group they are ungrateful, fickle, cowardly, and covetous, while individuals always maintain high standards of behavior. But as long as you can play on people's innate lack of self-esteem, they are yours entirely. They will offer you their blood, property, life, and children when the need is far distant, but when it approaches, they will turn against you unless you are extremely careful. Therefore, it is necessary to play on the emotions of citizens and workers, especially in dangerous times, and treat them like they were treated as children so that you sustain your culture and control of assets. People understand this method because they see their own behavior reflected in your governance.

An oligarch who relies entirely on promises and has neglected precautions is often ruined. Friendships obtained by bribes and not by great acts and nobility of ideas may indeed be earned, but they are not secure, and when needed are not reliable. But if people see that clemency and cruelty are dependent on conditions, they learn to wait to be told in the media about those conditions. Meanwhile, your plans can unfold.

Oligarchic control of media can be relied on to spin information in a way to make even cruel acts plausible. Eighty percent of global media are controlled as of this writing by seven companies: News Corp, Bertelsmann, Viacom, Disney, Time Warner, Vivendi, and Sony. This concentration, paid for by collaboration with other corporations and donations to governments worldwide, is vulnerable to incursions from Google, Apple, Facebook, and other electronic media firms such as Comcast seeking to displace them.

Again, the chief risk to hegemony is conflict among oligarchs and disruption of their networks.

The news and social media isolate individual situations from their context, such as the government removal of the rancher, Cliven Bundy, from protesting public lands without reporting that he had been grazing his animals there for free. The media reinforce the illusion of individual freedom isolated from the social fabric through examples that correspond to the consumerism that pays media salaries. Conservative media promote antigovernment politicians, so the ire of people is increased beyond the ability of the media to staunch their anger. The Trump administration and Brexit are the downstream effects of stoking such emotions. Vague ideals like freedom are preferred to specific principles like the balance between freedom and equality. The former can always be relied on to support strong reactions about independence, while the latter can be spun by antagonists as a threat to someone and by that fear generate resistance. You must remember, however, that the principle of balance is essential to running all organizations and must be the target you use to make most decisions.

The oligarch must understand that different situations require diverse actions and attitudes. Managing your triple role as lawmaker, law enforcer, and apparently law-abiding citizen remains a key skill in maintaining the loyalty of citizens and employees. If leadership fails to recognize the complex relationships inherent in this triple role, disaffection and ultimately the breakdown of society results, even with the support of the media, as was shown in North Africa during the Arab Spring.

Nevertheless, the oligarchic network, by using law, security forces, and media spin, inspires fear and anxiety in such a way that, if it does not win love, it avoids hatred. It can endure being feared when it is not hated. Popular entertainment produced by so-called Hollywood liberals actually reinforces feelings of persecution and fear of reprisal from a powerful, unseen network. This sanguine condition will continue as long as an oligarch abstains from unjustly taking the property of others. When it is necessary to proceed against someone, you must do it with proper justification and for manifest cause in line with the current laws, phrases, and protestations of fairness through the network, rather than taking action directly.

Above all, the oligarch must avoid appropriating the property of others, because men more quickly forget the death of their fathers than the loss of their patrimony. For example, second-generation Chinese reds currently in power, including Xi Jinping, use phrases like "red beliefs," "kingdom consciousness," and "big picture consciousness" to defend their support of the regime that persecuted and in some cases caused the death of their parents. The son of Liu Shaoqi, the former chairman of China during the Cultural Revolution, was persecuted to death by Mao's regime. With the help of his wife's excellent diplomacy, his own son, Liu Yuan, is now an army general who is on good terms with Xi Jinping and the next generation of the party leaders. Liu Yuan is poised to become the most powerful military leader in China. While Mao deserved their anger for being responsible for the deaths of their parents, contemporary Chinese leaders say that those who drink water should be grateful for its origin. Nevertheless, well-mediated appropriation of the property of workers and citizens can often be disguised as financial prudence, such as in the destruction of defined benefit pension plans and the proposed reduction in the US of Social Security and Medicare benefits by Republicans. The same kind of claw back of an oligarch's assets and contracts can only be accomplished in instances of criminal behavior.

Through media networks, the oligarch can also generate an emotional pretext, like reducing the size of oppressive government, to disguise this theft of citizens' and workers' property. The oligarchic network can make big government look like a tyrannical father because many people will transfer their rage at their fathers to that government. Besides, pretexts for taking away property are never wanting. A group of politicians who live by robbing their citizens will always find reasons for seizing what belongs to others. And here control of the courts and media becomes important as we have already said.

Among the cruel deeds attributed to Reagan in order to bolster his strong-man image was the claim that he destroyed the Soviet Union. But he did not. The Soviet Union was a failing state by the late '70s and had always had a weak economy. Soviet leaders such as Edward Shevardnadze, Alexander Yakovlev, and Gorbachev negotiated the retreat from Marxism against hardliners in the oligarchy. Does anyone know what they promised the leaders of factories and regions to gain their support? Reagan simply made it appear that he was the cause of the Soviet demise by using the media to advantage. And Trump is already taking credit for prosperity resulting from the policies of the Obama administration.

Simultaneously, Reagan falsely claimed to have reduced the size of government like a true conservative, but in fact, he increased government spending and reduced taxes on the wealthy so that the debt increased. He disguised increased debt as economic growth. In fact, Reagan's was the first administration to escalate the consumer debt-driven economy that has by now capped growth at low levels with the exception of the computer revolution that resulted in real growth. Such is the strength of oligarchic networks that government is still being criticized for providing benefits to the people. Many voters, due to emotions driven by media disinformation, applaud being stripped of their own pensions and especially those of their neighbors. The US continues to suffer from the corporate takeover of government, privatizing gains, and converting private losses to public debt.

As we have mentioned, cheerful sincerity makes a civil leader attractive to both the people and the funders. This attribute made Reagan revered by the people. But without his apparent cruelty toward the Soviets, his other virtues were insufficient to produce this effect and hide the wholesale theft of creating the consumer debt economy. He is known for firing unionized air traffic controllers, an action that had a strong effect on public opinion. His bullying and opportunism in Grenada, coming just a day or two after 240 Marines were killed in Lebanon, knocked that story off the top of the front page. Finally, we can't blame him that much either because he was not the leader of any of those initiatives that are attributed to him. Rather Reagan acted as the pawn and cohort of the conservative networks of the security state, oil patch, and other industries, and he was from the first an informant for law enforcement.

Returning to the question of being feared or loved, we come to the conclusion that, people, loving according to their own desire and fearing because of the actions of leadership, the oligarch should be both feared and loved to take advantage of both individual desire and the control you have over people who are fearful. Wise CEOs or civil leaders should use what is accessible and under their control and not controlled by others. The oligarch must endeavor only to avoid hatred. Almost all other behavior can be papered over with media spin.

Chapter XVIII: Concerning the Way in Which Oligarchs Should Keep Faith

Everyone admires oligarchs who keep their word, abide by signed contracts and treaties, and who live more with integrity than by craft. Nevertheless, leaders who have done great things have not put much value on promises. They ignore contracts when they think they can do so without significant impact to their business and break treaties when those relationships no longer support their policies. They have known how to circumvent the intellect of men by shrewdness and in the end overcome those who relied on their word.

There are three ways of disputing—by law, by resistance, and by force. When the first doesn't work, oligarchs have recourse to the third. The second is the main option of the people or when weaker oligarchs are attacked by stronger ones. Therefore, an oligarch must engage both the rational faculties and the emotional triggers of subordinates, since both are contained in each person. People are convinced when they think that they are the source of an idea. War made many leaders famous such as Julius Caesar, Mao Zedong, George Washington, Napoleon Bonaparte, Genghis Khan, and Arjuna, so you should know how to manage both kinds of behavior in others and yourself. Emotion without reason and vice versa are unsustainable, as arbitrary emotions often appear abhorrent and rationality often appears stilted.

Subtle combinations of reason and emotion link the senses to emergent properties like inventiveness and loyalty, while the *cul de sac* of binaries creates internecine squabbles and environmental problems. Pretending that humans can completely rise above their animal or physical nature undermines the essential *détente* between humanity and the rest of the biosphere. Identifying humans exclusively as animals loses the attention of individual egos. Until science captures human thought in a test tube, we continue to rely on the many complex relationships between our rational selves, our emotional and neurological reactions, and the influences of our surroundings. As an oligarch you must deal with all these components in determining how to act even if you don't think about them overtly. Some leaders will carefully map out each component before acting. Others will operate by the seat of their pants or gut feel, as Americans say, referring to the second largest complex of neurons in the body located in the abdomen adjacent to the digestive tract's cache of bacteria.

When compelled knowingly to adopt a violent response, an oligarch should choose both the fox and the lion, since the lion cannot defend itself against snares, and the fox cannot defend itself against wolves. Those who rely simply on the lion do not understand what they are doing, and foxes often find themselves in the position of Julien Sorel, having been too smart for their own good.

As a savvy leader, you need not keep faith when it may be turned against you, and when the reasons that caused you to pledge it no longer exist. If humanity were entirely consistent and living in a static world, this principle would not hold, but because both the people and the world are constantly changing, they will not always keep faith with you. You are not obligated either, although you will want to promote that behavior in other people. Neither will an oligarch need legitimate reasons to excuse nonobservance. On this point, endless modern examples could be given, showing how many treaties and contracts have been voided through the faithlessness of leaders and manipulation through the courts. Simply remembering how in the example already discussed in earlier chapters that workers' pension obligations have been ignored, obviated, re-engineered, and litigated by corporations and municipalities in the US, leaving workers without the security that they have paid for, should be proof enough. The vagaries of foreign treaties for all nations seals the evidence.

Contract law in most successful nations is so important to the operations of an oligarch's network that these promises can only be broken if the law is not invoked, or if negotiation or donations to the proper coffers place the law on the network's side. Again, the bankruptcy of Detroit and the wholesale change of US worker pensions from defined benefit plans to defined contribution plans, or cancelling them altogether, makes even carefully written contracts subject to the vagaries of law and changing conditions. Even when lawyers get involved, independent relations between management and workers are finally based on trust.

Returning to the question of keeping faith, Obama after many protestations and agreements with other Democrats to avoid drilling for oil in the Arctic suddenly agreed to allow drilling on the Alaska North Slope by Shell Oil. The Audubon Society has documented six visits to the White House by Shell's President, Marvin Odum, prior to the change of policy, which showed the power of oligarchic connections. The irony, of course, was that Shell didn't find any oil. The issue of energy independence appears to have driven Obama's acquiescence.

Obama, after pledging to stop companies from shipping US jobs overseas, promoted the Trans-Pacific Partnership in which national laws can be overridden by international trade agreements that are controlled and adjudicated by corporate lawyers, selling out not only his country's workers, but its laws and sovereignty as well. Most current calculations show that the number of new jobs created by TPP would only equal the number of jobs lost, with benefits going to corporations and their leaders on both sides of the ocean. The actual justification for TPP is limiting China's sphere of influence. Trump and Wilbur Ross have cancelled further negotiations of TPP.

CHAPTER XVIII: CONCERNING THE WAY IN WHICH OLIGARCHS SHOULD KEEP... 97

If and once global government is installed, agreements such as TPP will be hailed as groundbreaking. The global capital network controls and suborns administrators like presidents. The network's support is assumed to be necessary to run any government and pay for elections, but in the absence of progressive taxation, government income is less dependent on the richest people and more on the overall population. On the other hand, electoral politics are controlled in the US by those richest individuals who no longer have to pay such a large proportion of state budgets. The US courts have created a false equivalence of money with speech to assure sustainability of this felicitous arrangement for the oligarch.

Current laws address the first amendment of the US Constitution in fragments, only as separable individual rights rather than also for its sense as an interdependent social contract that includes religions, press, speech, assembly, and petition of government. Oligarchs should note how this fragmentation strategy can be applied to citizens, yet avoided by leadership networks.

Corporate leaders, anticipating the effects of fragmentation, have reneged on their multigenerational commitments to maintain a secure retirement for their workers, saying that it was too expensive. In fact, it was through mismanagement of pension funds and rent-seeking for personal gain that drove corporate leaders to turn firms' obligations into worker responsibilities, as if workers could possibly manage their retirement funds as well as CFOs and pension specialists trained for years to manage money. Not coincidentally, the lost funds end up being paid as fees to investment banks, among whose shareholders number those same CFOs and pension managers. There are more examples, such as Social Security surpluses used to bolster government deficits, but do leaders suffer the consequences of such betrayal and faithlessness? Therefore, while it makes sense to posture that faith is a characteristic of great leadership, an oligarch knows that you will frequently change rules and laws for tactical reasons, remembering that you want your workers and citizens to believe that their commitments to you are binding.

It is also necessary to know how to pretend reliability while maintaining a cheerful exterior. People want to be persuaded because they are often in insecure positions and anxious about the future, looking to leadership for security. Income inequality makes them increasingly vulnerable to current everyday necessities. So, an oligarch who seeks to deceive will always find people who will allow themselves to be deceived. This was true for oligarchs like Bush and Cheney who lied and encouraged others like General Colin Powell, viewed as a paragon of trustworthiness, to lie about the necessity of invading Iraq. The lies of the Trump administration are continuous, but his followers forgive him. Media hoaxes on talk radio blatantly misrepresent facts to appeal to their listeners' biases that have been fostered by continual repetition of the form of honesty. Again, we must question form when it is inconsistent with how things operate. In the larger frame, all complex systems lack uniformity due to developing over time with a dependence on conditions that often change moment to moment.

A similar bias is true for our identity-oriented culture. This code, promoted by oligarchic networks, teaches the people to revel in spontaneous perception and immediate reactions. It encourages us all to believe that our feelings, rather than a combination of self-interest, sensibility, and rationality, are the key operational components of any exchange. In actual practice, however, people in most conditions see the world dynamically and alter their views many times a day as their role changes and as their interests also inescapably change. Identity culture as promoted by corporate public relations and advertising fails to acknowledge the daily rebalancing of perspectives that occur for each individual. It is relegated to trumpeting past victories and heroes. It claims every person's situation is unique and univocal. More to the point, individual and group identities are built over time in layers. These layers are accessed conditionally, with those retrieved most frequently either from pain or aspiration remaining near the surface of our consciousness.

From another point of view, humans are all similar in our uniqueness, knowing each other by our differences as much as by our similarities. There will always be thought leaders who say what they want people to hear and how they think people want to hear it. We become afraid of disagreement and thereby repressive. However, our political and economic ecosystems operate in a constantly shifting and complex framework that is difficult to predict and which cannot be understood by a succession of platitudes, binaries, and one-liners. Everybody truly knows this already, but a set of convincing principles that does not rely on control by a few has not been devised to impress these environmental facts on the people. Perhaps climate change promotes cultural change; perhaps it also promotes continuing increasingly unequal oligarchy without close attention to environmental justice.

Those who think people are ignorant should be viewed skeptically, no matter what their position, because they are planning to lead you astray. It is not that people are ignorant, but that the world is very complex and full of uncertainties. The human desire to have reality simply outlined, whole and complete, as we sense our organism to be, one with our identity, may be interpreted by the effective oligarch as a sign that the people on our planet

CHAPTER XVIII: CONCERNING THE WAY IN WHICH OLIGARCHS SHOULD KEEP... 99

do not perceive themselves as they are. Except when something is obvious, only those who avoid simplifying should be trusted. Even then, one should examine their motives in saying so, as complexity can be used like fog to disguise self-interest. It would be nice if our surroundings were easier to understand, but they are not.

It is impossible for an oligarch to have all the good qualities people expect from leadership, but it is necessary to appear to have them. We dare say, too, that to have them and always to observe them is injurious. Although heroes and saints are continually held up to have had them, people did not like the behavior of the irascible Mother Teresa, along with other grumpy saints and bullying heroes. But to appear to have these good qualities is useful. To appear merciful, faithful, humane, religious, upright, and to ordinarily be so, but with a mind so framed that you do not need to be so, cannot in fact constantly be so, remains the most auspicious functional behavior for an oligarch. You must be able and know how to change to the opposite, to some tangent, or to some altogether different framework. This flexibility helps you balance short- and long-term goals with an eye toward taking as few risks as possible to achieve those goals. In this way, whatever happens, you have another chance.

By now you understand that an oligarch, especially a new one such as a newly elected leader or promoted CEO, cannot observe all those virtues for which people are esteemed. You will be often forced to act contrary to faith, friendship, humanity, and religion, in order to maintain the state or the bottom line and to minimize existing power bases that may be hostile to your intentions within your organization. All these apparent and actual behaviors are inherent in leadership.

It is necessary, therefore, to fix your mind on your goals and, according to need, focus on the direction of the winds and variations of conditions to maintain your position in the network. Even these changes cannot follow any narrow ethics, not even self-interest narrowly framed, since policy must be changed as infrequently as possible to preserve the illusion that you follow the moral precepts that workers and citizens have been taught to support. As mentioned, you should not diverge from the good if you can avoid doing so, but, if compelled, you must know how do it while appearing not to have done so.

For this reason, you ought to take care to never let anything slip from your lips that is not replete with the above-named good qualities so that you may appear altogether supportive, merciful, faithful, humane, upright, green, pious, and tough. In our world, today, when religion arises everywhere in resistance to and in imitation of bathetic corporate culture, these last two qualities are vital.

People judge you more by the eye than by the hand because everybody sees you in the media, but few come in touch with you. Everyone sees what you appear to be, while few know what you really are, as in the cases of John Kennedy or Reagan, who were as men far removed from their public personae. The higher you go, the more distant you are from your people, so you need, therefore, to take measures always to keep in touch with their needs, especially those of your colleagues whom you expect to implement your programs.

You can take this position: the few who are in touch with you dare not oppose the opinion of the masses that you have already fostered in them, lest you expose these few as traitors, impious, or simply not doing their jobs. Yet you must be careful how this is done, or your judgement may be brought into doubt for having so many faithless and incompetent ministers and executives, even you, who has the majesty of the corporation and state defending you. For the actions of all people, and especially of oligarchs, are ultimately judged by outcomes, even if at first you can create a screen of emotions and rhetoric to convince people about your intentions. Realizations about results often take a long time to percolate, but they do rise to the surface. Too-frequent appeal to higher authorities like the state, the corporation, or the deity brings your authority into question in the long run although, in the short run, changing the framework while appearing consistent has always been the practical method of oligarchy.

For that reason, an oligarch ought to take credit for winning and maintaining the corporation or the state. Even if your victories depend on your cohorts, you must treat the assertions of this book as questionable. Your means will usually be considered justified at some level. As an example, people still give money to banks to save and invest, even when, like Barclay's and other major banks, they were convicted of colluding to manipulate interest rates. This is a complexity trap. Oligarchs will be praised by everybody because the media can be taken in by what seems to be and rarely look into events in detail, except for a few outlets.

We are all convinced by outcomes while constantly judging surfaces. In the media world, there are for the most part those who are convinced of the rhetoric of oligarchy and those who are out of power. A few journalists find a place through their network, while most no longer have any career to rest on, which is why we have the concept of equality of opportunity built into all major democracies and never in the case of corporations or totalitarian states. Here we speak supportively of form, comparing income inequality in the US to Singapore, where it is much higher, to show that there is some value to the people in democratic form.

Many leaders in the US and the EU today never preach anything but peace and good faith, and yet they are hostile to both. If they had kept the peace and faith with the people, they would have been frequently deprived of their reputation, their offices, and their holdings. This is so because a strong organization, either national or corporate, depends on singular people who understand their differences and similarities, the expectation of reciprocity in social engagements, and their working community. The oligarchy inevitably fosters these three forces, but cannot always function within the ethics they imply. Learning to operate through this complex network remains the skill of oligarchs.

Chapter XIX: That One Should Avoid Being Despised and Hated

As an oligarch, you must consider how to avoid what will make you hated or contemptible. Insofar as you succeed, you should not fear rebuke. Above all, it will make you hated, as we have said, to be rapacious and to violate the property rights of the families of your employees and citizens. When neither their property nor honor is touched, the majority of people live contentedly. The ambition of other oligarchs can be controlled in many ways, and among them are respect for their achievements and acknowledgement of their domains.

An oligarch will be despised if considered fickle, frivolous, mean-spirited, waffling, and irresolute, all of which you should guard against as from a sharp stick in the eye. You should endeavor to show in your actions greatness, courage, gravity, and fortitude. In your private dealings with citizens and employees, you should show that your judgements are data-driven rather than fixed, so that you can change direction as conditions change without being accused of flip-flopping. You must offer benefits to your network while reducing risk by changing only when necessary, because the unintended consequences of change appear as a major risk to power.

In dealings with your network, you must always be respectful and appear to support the group's interests. You must maintain a reputation that no one can either deceive you or get around you as Trump postured throughout his campaign. Presenting himself in this way, he may be undermined by libertarians who themselves can manipulate conditions that force him to change while appearing blameless themselves. This is why, with global population approaching eight billion, understanding how to manage complexity and probability have become so important. Managing complexity means that you must maintain several scenarios rather than a single inflexible plan, because prediction remains difficult especially further into the future. Appreciating how your network operates, how information and power are transmitted across it, is as important as understanding yourself and those near you. Understanding only the individual people and not the character of their interactions makes it impossible to control your own actions. Admitting and appreciating the level of independence of those interactions is difficult and a key skill of an effective oligarch.

As an oligarch, you are esteemed when you convey an impression of stability. Provided people consider you an excellent person and revere you, you may only be attacked or intimidated with difficulty. For this reason, you ought to watch three groups for possible betrayal: your employees and citizens, external powers, and those of your peers who might have designs on your assets and connections. With all these possible adversaries, the current dispute between globalists and nationalists is far from ended.

We have covered the first and the second groups in discussing how you must manage yourself and your domain. Even when affairs outside are disturbed, if one has carefully prepared and has operated as indicated, unless one despairs, every attack can be resisted as the Venetians did for 1400 years.

From the third, you can protect yourself with contingency plans and good connections, by doing favors for your peers, knowing when they are stressed, and making sure you understand their interests and goals as much as possible, as well as why they need certain connections. In this way, you can accommodate them without decreasing your own wealth and power. You are often served by taking a subordinate position in a deal to maintain your assets while another oligarch takes the lead. Trump understands the value of limited partnerships and licensing only his name.

As Hamilton said in *Federalist IX*, "A firm Union will be of the utmost moment to the peace and liberty of the States, as a barrier against domestic faction and insurrection." Here we see one of the leading oligarchs among the US's founding fathers clearly stating how domestic factions do not serve the body politic. By promoting factions, Trump fails to unify the focus of the country. An oligarch establishes a firm union by providing for the needs of citizens, employees, and the fraternal network. In resisting

CHAPTER XIX: THAT ONE SHOULD AVOID BEING DESPISED AND HATED 103

oppression, the first task of an aspiring oligarch is to understand how to reduce factionalism among potential allies in changing the status quo.

Unless you give ridiculous advantage to cronies and direct supporters, everyone will allow you some level of favoritism, so long as appearances are maintained. But power dangerously declared itself in the case of Citizens United v. FEC, which appears to lock in control of public elections by allowing unlimited financing by oligarchs and corporate interests. These litigants, however, may in the end have precipitated the downfall of conservative leadership, because they breached the veil, revealing their mechanisms of control that had worked well for most of two centuries with few successful insurrections. This break in democratic form and plausible deniability may have been a turning point, pushing the people and those oligarchs not currently in power to promote more transparency in governance. The cut-rate victory of Trump in 2016 supports this point, although he now attempts to align his administration with libertarian and conservative establishments. The saving grace for existing oligarchs is that media power is so great that almost any breach can be papered over by keeping media in the network. What appears to be a major hole in the illusions of governance may in the end be spun as a minor adjustment, but the jury is still out.

When the networks of the state have been disturbed and possibly realigned as with Trump's victory, the network has to fear that outsiders, like Putin, will conspire secretly with those within. An oligarch can best be secured from conspiracy by avoiding being hated and despised, by keeping the people satisfied, and by giving no offense to network peers, since the difficulties that confront the conspirator are infinite.

While there have been many conspiracies, few have been successful. Those who conspire can rarely act alone or take companions except those that they believe to be dissatisfied. As soon as you have opened your mind to malcontents, you give them the ammunition to empower themselves, since by denouncing you they can gain advantage. Expecting assured improvement from betrayal and seeing the path of your conspiracy to be risky, your co-conspirator must be a rare friend indeed, or a thoroughly obstinate enemy of current leadership, to maintain faith with you.

To reduce the scope of this issue, we maintain that, on the side of the conspirator or hostile takeover, there is fear, jealousy, and the prospect of punishment to terrify. But on the side of the oligarch in power there is the dignity of the state and corporation, the law, and the protection of friends and relatives as bulwark. Adding popular goodwill, it is improbable that anyone would be so rash as to conspire or seek to take over the well-defended corporation. For in general, the conspirator is afraid before the execution of the plot. The conspirator also fears the crime's sequel because now the people are an enemy. Yet many a CEO regrets relying too heavily on the form of the corporation, the corporate veil that protects individuals within the corporation, and ignoring shareholders and operations as beneath notice.

Endless corporate examples could be given on this subject, but we will be content with one. Jerry Levin, CEO of Time Warner, contemplated an internal takeover of Time Warner's 24-hour CNN news channel. Contrary to historical stories of insurrections where one oligarch fights another, preserving the illusion of competition, Ted Turner thought Levin's takeover was a pretty good idea. But implementation of the takeover was stymied by other leaders of Time Warner who didn't want their divisional powers compromised by Levin's proposed changes. In the end, Levin had to buy Steve Case and Ted Leonsis' AOL because of the hostility of his own confreres.

The unpredictability of evolving technology shows why countries like Russia and China fear the Internet destabilizing their regimes. They have the Arab Spring as an example of how changing the linkages of network nodes produced volatile results, for these relationships are the basis of power. The more connections an oligarch has within the subnet, the more power is available to them at different times and for different purposes. An oligarch must control local ecosystems to be sure of the support of internal forces. Further, oligarchs cannot be sure that external forces do not replace their bases of power as the printing press, gun powder, internal combustion engines, electricity, and semiconductors have overthrown oligarchies throughout history.

For these reasons, you shouldn't worry about conspiracies when your subordinates and peers hold you in esteem and support your strategies. But when they are hostile to you and external forces, such as technological change, occur, you ought to fear everything and everyone. Well-ordered states and companies must take care not to drive either leading citizens or middle management to despair and to keep the people satisfied and contented whenever possible.

Factionalism remains dangerous to an oligarch's control. The global oligarch must seek to avoid factions among key global players such as large trading nations, banks, and multinational corporations, since they make network management more difficult and block the connections to

CHAPTER XIX: THAT ONE SHOULD AVOID BEING DESPISED AND HATED   105

resources such as rare earths and experts in specialized domains. As a countervailing force, complex bureaucracy strengthens both the state and the corporation even if managing these larger organizations costs more. Larger entities are also more resilient to environmental challenges such as drought, labor costs, and reduced demand for goods and services. Every important empire has used bureaucracy to slow change, even as change continues. On the other hand, factions empower local oligarchs and leaders who divide their opponents, since smaller organizations such as counties, provinces, companies that profit from a local geography, and fragmented opposition are easier and cheaper to control than large nations and global corporations. Conservative efforts to empower smaller government are driven by this desire to fragment the state, but even they must avoid factions in their localities to insure the ease of controlling small groups.

Among the best-ordered and governed oligarchies of our times is Germany with its corporations. Germany contains many strong institutions and leaders, from Chancellor Angela Merkel to the boards of Allianz, E.ON, and Volkswagen. Bundestag authority has a liberal bias, since liberal bias restored it after WWII. Since the colonial ambitions of German corporate oligarchs were thwarted by Allied oligarchs between the wars, the Germans were emboldened to start WWII. Afterwards, the Bundestag included these corporations in the reconstituted network since reconstruction required their support.

The Bundestag knew how to share the network's wealth with German citizens. The country was reconstituted with worker security and the trappings of freedom partly through the example of the Marshall Plan and partly to divert workers from the attractions of Communism. In fact, anything was better than what went before. The Bundestag used the culture of freedom to avoid making corporate leaders jealous of keeping labor's wages and benefits high. It promoted forgiveness among the people and favored the oligarchs by not throwing them all in jail for supporting the war. With help from the Marshall Plan, leadership set up a legal system that could manage the great and favor the lesser without reproach and while rebuilding the oligarchic network. There can be no more prudent arrangement or greater source of security to the oligarchs of states and corporations than a sustainable balance of power and wealth. Immigration from war and climate change now threatens that balance.

A perspicacious oligarch may draw another important conclusion from the German experience. Leave reproach to others and keep compassion in your own hands as Trump and Putin might learn. This justifies separation of powers in quite a different sense. Further, the oligarchy ought to include both corporations and citizens in appropriate capacities, to avoid making it hated by either or to pit them against each other more than necessary. Although shared power is more difficult to wield, it is, with prosperity, the best insurance against insurgency.

An orderly state contends only with the ambition of the corporations and the demands of the workers. But leadership also has, on the third hand, to deal with the cruelty and avarice of its security personnel, a faction so plagued with difficulties that it has ruined many organizations. It is extremely difficult to satisfy both the police and the people, because the people love peace and wish for the most part to be left alone. For this reason, they love the unaspiring oligarch. The police on the other hand love the bold and rapacious leader. They often choose to practice their craft on the people, especially the poor and any who appear different than the leadership. In fact, anyone different in appearance or behavior than the police themselves remains suspect. In this way police get double pay and exercise their penchant for cruelty in the face of the slightest resistance. Local leaders without bellicose or traditional authority are often undermined by the police.

Many new oligarchs, recognizing the conflict between the police and the poor, are inclined to satisfy the police, since no one wants to know what happens in the neighborhoods under cover of darkness. Thus, organizations like Black Lives Matter must shed light on inappropriate police behavior. These groups insure that injustice does not become a habit with the police, since once unchecked, violent behavior becomes habitual for many officers, uniformed or otherwise. As noted, the security state is responsible for atrocities in many nations. This violence exists as much in the presentation of ideas as in wielding the baton, as many who seek ideological reconciliation have discovered. People with ideas often defend them with as much vigor as a man defending his castle.

Such patterns also occur because local leaders are often hated, especially by those who did not vote for them. They represent an opposing authority or simply have different concerns. So, in order to avoid being hated by everyone, local oligarchs ought to avoid the hatred of the most powerful, that is, the business interests allied with the police who have been known defend property more than quality of life. Those local leaders, who, through inexperience, need special favors adhere more readily to the police than to the people.

Mayors of New York Bloomberg and Bill de Blasio are both modest leaders, enemies to cruelty, lovers of justice, humane, and benign, but of

CHAPTER XIX: THAT ONE SHOULD AVOID BEING DESPISED AND HATED   107

different temperaments regarding the exercise of authority. De Blasio ran into trouble with the police of New York because they were used to the license that Bloomberg gave them. In another case, Richard Daley of Chicago allowed the police to move forward against demonstrators and looters in 1968, saying, "I said to tell [superintendent James B. Conlisk] very emphatically and very definitely that an order be issued by him immediately to shoot to kill any arsonist or anyone with a Molotov cocktail in his hand, because they're potential murderers, and to shoot to maim or cripple anyone looting." While this caused a great deal of controversy in the press, exacerbated by the conflict over Viet Nam, Daley reigned over Chicago until his death in 1976. His son with similar policies rose to become mayor a few years afterward and led Chicago for an even longer period with the full support of the police against many citizens without repercussions significant enough to unseat him from office.

On the other hand, Perón, although he had the support of the people, could not maintain his country against a well-organized oligarchy allied with global commercial and security interests who thought they could only become rich by dominating a docile workforce. Due to this conflict with other oligarchs, the Perón regime in Argentina was more politically polarized than any since. The landowning elites, security forces, and other conservatives pushed him out of power three times. Three times the people put him back in power, before employers and moderates generally agreed with the conservatives to keep the peace. These changes occurred in spite of the fact that the economy had grown by over 40 percent under Perón, far exceeding the global growth rate.

This example shows the power of oligarchy not only in rent seeking but also in the security and control that characterize their networks. The underprivileged, populists, and humanitarians look back on Perón's era differently. Real wages grew by over a third and better working conditions arrived alongside benefits like pensions, health care, paid vacations, and the construction of record numbers of needed schools, hospitals, housing, and other infrastructure. Nevertheless, without the support of other oligarchs and the security forces, Perón fell again and again.

Argentina has been a hotbed of corruption ever since, culminating in the kleptocracy of Cristina Fernández de Kirchner who, in spite of her self-dealing, retained the support of police and the army even against the objections of global capital. This example shows how networks become strong through many connections that are well maintained by upright citizens, business groups, security forces, and traditional political alliances.

We will end this discussion by pointing out that oligarchs in our times of high population density give inordinate satisfaction to security forces, having expanded the security state beyond any in history. Since Napoleon, leadership has felt the need for powerful secretive policing, including bulk surveillance of citizens' communications to protect the network from the increasing power of individuals and small groups.

Most people never knew that they were being watched until Julian Assange's WikiLeaks and Edward Snowden exposed the unwarranted storage of nearly every electronic communication. This data storage conflicted with the US Constitution, creating uncertainty and disagreement that threatened oligarchic governance. Once exposed, Obama had to bolster his administration with factions he would have preferred to leave out of his government, such as oil producers. Further he had to include those who, through the TPP and other trade agreements, would ship jobs overseas to reduce corporate labor costs, although Obama probably was leaning that way from the beginning. One may doubt Trump's promises about trade deals, but one cannot doubt the sustained power of the security state through concepts from mutually assured destruction through surveillance using the Internet of things.

6: On the Projects of Oligarchs

CHAPTER XX: ARE BUILDING PROGRAMS, WALLS, FORTRESSES, AND OTHER PROJECTS TO WHICH OLIGARCHS OFTEN RESORT ADVANTAGEOUS OR BURDENSOME?

1. Some oligarchs, to secure the state, have disarmed their citizens. Others have armed them all, building citizen armies to reduce the cost of standing armies. Others have controlled their subordinates in both corporations and nations by creating factions among them. Still others have diverted enemies by manipulating them to fight each other. Others have organized their security forces to monitor those they distrusted while they secured the reins of power. Some retain those surveillance regimes as long as they can afford them. Some have built skyscrapers, walls, and fortresses; some have overthrown and destroyed them. Each of these tactics may be useful under certain conditions and each must be addressed in context. The notion that one strategy is both workable and ethical under all conditions doesn't support the need of an oligarch to remain nimble.

2. Although princes and conquerors disarm those they have defeated, as a new oligarch you can't disarm the citizens or disenfranchise your employees and expect a good result. (Reorganizing corporations and nations for globalization modifies this statement, and we'll discuss that soon.) When you find people disarmed or powerless within an organization, you may arm them or at least seem to empower them by loudly promoting ideas they agree with. By arming them, promoting their morals, and giving them new technologies, their arms and skills become yours. Those people who were

distrusted become faithful, and those who were faithful remain so. In this way citizens and employees become supporters.

When you give your workers new computers and arm your citizens or, even better for the economy and your budget, allow them to arm themselves with weapons they desire, all benefit, although there may be collateral damage. Today all employees and citizens can be given new technology due to the low cost of computers (in most industries less than 3 percent of revenues) and/or armed with rifles. (We shall see how this oversupply impacts oligarchic control.) Both the unarmed and unarmed are controlled with television and the Internet, which depict the use of guns in many emotionally satisfying situations. The presence or absence of weapons remains less important than prioritizing a culture of violence over negotiation, since those values divert people from participating and competing in the exercise of power.

In the case of armaments, the objections of pacifists can be incorporated into a moral code that minimizes gun control, assuring that the state retains a monopoly on power. The conflict about gun control is then understood as a political difference of opinion. It is fought in the legislatures and in the press, sidelining questions about the powers accorded leadership. And arms sales continue to strengthen the economy. Meanwhile popular media continue to promote violence and the cult of individualism without negative consequences for them because they make money that way.

In addition, the oligarchy gains a strong adherent by including the arms manufacturers in its network. The revolutionary bourgeoisie has had two effects. In the first place, oligarchs support each other in capitalist society, instead of fighting as in Machiavelli's day, because civil oligarchy protects private property. Corporate competition is rarely monolithic and usually takes the form of coopetition, as in the technology field, and the turf is clearly divided as among electric utilities. (The introduction of renewable energy raises a specter for the power companies.) Second, the middle class has been empowered by paper currency and easy credit to enrich lenders to the extent their income allows. And often, even if their income doesn't support a loan, regulations can assure that debtors can't escape obligations through declaring bankruptcy the same way a corporation can.

An oligarch must be cautious, however, not to take too much away from citizens and workers because the oligarch actually benefits from their well-being. The greater the level of income equality, the richer the country overall. Inequality promotes disengagement from markets, but more radical activity at the polling place, as we saw in the US and UK in 2016. Oligarchs seeking to only maximize their wealth fail to understand this ecology of economies.

If as an oligarch, you attempt to disarm all citizens because of the fear of social unrest and increased murder rates or disloyalty, your distrust offends everybody. Since any justification for disarming your citizens breeds anger in some sectors of the population, you must decide who you can afford to offend. Usually workers and citizens are less responsive to loss of privileges than your fellow oligarchs, but if they are both physically attacked and impoverished, they will organize against visible powers.

An armed citizenry benefits leadership as long as the culture promotes reciprocity and collaboration. An empowered workforce is excited by the new tools and focuses its attention on the job at hand. But if the oligarch promotes factions among citizens and also arms them, the society becomes volatile, to the detriment of the oligarchy that benefits from continued peace for business growth. Such conditions exist in the US today and threaten civility between classes. Some leaders in minor states use these strategies to maintain power with armed militias, but imitating weak dictators in places like Honduras or the Philippines does not add to the legacy of developed and enlightened states.

In the other case, when an oligarch acquires a state or company, adding a province or division to an existing one, then it is necessary to disarm the citizens of that new province and to reorganize the employees of the acquired company, in order that old alliances cannot conspire against you, as in the Deutsche Bank example discussed earlier. The exception must be those individuals who have assisted in acquiring the new organization. With time and opportunity, acquired workers should be organized around the company's culture or retrained to be productive.

Some corporations bring in new leadership to move jobs overseas and to fire redundant employees for the purposes of making additional profit. This approach alienates the employees from the corporation and makes for a conflicted work environment even more so than the norm. Companies that follow this practice do so to their long-term disadvantage, in spite of what consultants tell us about strategy.

Globalization benefits financial and labor-intensive industries by creating an oversupply of workers. This imbalance lowers demand within each country and leads to stagnation while temporarily increasing corporate profits. Fiscal stimulus, more than monetary stimulus, needs to be applied to increase demand. Building roads and bridges, power grids and solar farms acts initially as a small tax on the oligarchy, but it should be done or society again will become politically volatile and economically stagnant, as when oligarchs promote factionalism.

The key to success of a global oligarch, as opposed to the local one, is to make borders more porous to capital flows and less porous to flows of people, unless they are associated, as are tourists, with capital flows. Immigration must be controlled, while at the same time you must appear to relieve human suffering in the wars caused by factionalism. The local oligarch has a very different agenda, needing cheap labor onshore. The global oligarch benefits from cheap labor offshore.

The struggle between global and local priorities has become the most difficult conflict to resolve as it drives people apart, distracts from reducing the volatility created by inequality, and makes addressing climate change that threatens all leadership more difficult. The ability to manage these complexities separates the successful oligarch from the short-term conquest of lands and wealth.

3. The uses of factionalism: The British Empire often managed its colonies like Arabia through factions. After WWI, the British wanted to control the Iraqi state because oil was more profitable when negotiating with a weak government. Consolidating British control of trade, the Lynch Steamship Company won a monopoly on trade on the Tigris and similar licenses were awarded at key control points of the economy. Taking over these strategic links in the network broke the power of the tribal leaders, setting them against each other and against the central government, so that they were distracted from attacking the British. Those in the weakened central government were then easily bribed to support the British policy. Finally, knowledgeable people like Gertrude Bell, British political officer and archeologist, were excluded from decision-making once the interests of finance dominated.

In another example of the use of factions, after WWII, US diplomat George F. Kenan and others developed a policy to contain the Soviet Union with massive deployments of tanks and missiles along the Iron Curtain. His strategy forced the Soviet Union to spend so much money on defense that by 1989 its empire was bankrupt. Pitting Russia's defense industry against spending on its citizens' well-being worked well throughout the post-WWII period. The US, being wealthier overall, was able to buy both guns and butter, although not without some internal conflict, strengthening the political and economic position of the defense industry.

CHAPTER XX: ARE BUILDING PROGRAMS, WALLS, FORTRESSES, AND OTHER... 113

Such a delicate policy was appropriate in those times when interests within the US were reasonably balanced. But it is unacceptable today. A united front to opposing nations fails today at many points as a result of factionalism in US leadership between those seeking global and those seeking local control. Corporate leaders in financial and resources companies and political leaders on both the right and the left are more intent on supporting their factions than on building a strong nation that would benefit both factions. Left and right support different foreign states. For example, Trump, with multiple local interests in real estate, seeks to support Russia and Israel, while Obama focused on China and other global economic alliances.

Oligarchs continue to benefit from factions in both government and business while the workers and middle class lose out. Profit increases for both oligarchic factions, although more so for globalists, since they agree that middle class wages should be driven down and inflation be limited to those products and services most used by the middle class and the poor—food, clothing, and shelter. Factionalism is focused on the behavior of the middle class and poor, driving a wedge through society under the aegis of social media and the 24-hour news cycle, making all individual affect offensive to someone.

The US's current factions have become so divided that a consistent and appropriate policy toward Iran, for example, cannot be adopted. One faction thinks it is more important to undermine the other faction than to present a common front. Supporters of Israel in both parties sought to derail Kerry and Obama's nuclear negotiations with Iran and made the settlement weaker. Machiavelli railed against factions, saying, it is certain that when the enemy comes upon you in divided cities, you are quickly lost. The weakest party will always assist the outside forces, and the stronger will not be able to resist attacks from inside and outside the country. The US begins to see that happening today when communities are torn by class and race, and Russia and China gain turf.

Efficient solutions to the problem of factions are implemented by corporations like IBM. When IBM takes over another technology company, it "blue washes" the acquired firm, which means modifying the systems of the new division to look as much like existing IBM systems as possible, homogenizing the culture. But when a new company is purchased, because it has better systems than the acquiring company, both systems are run parallel for many months until the new one is proven. This approach is expensive and only pays off over the long haul. Nevertheless, such a policy reduces factionalism and may be applied to political factions through appropriate public relations programs, although not without conflicts between oligarchic factions such as the Koch brothers' libertarian alliances, neoliberal globalists, and the remaining adherents of the New Deal's support for workers.

Another corporate solution may be relevant to political factionalism. In large companies, each division is periodically reorganized by seeding core executives into the new division and splitting up teams. In this way, the acquiring company's culture is maintained throughout the corporation and subnets are integrated into the whole. The US Congress and EU parliaments do not have such a cleansing process available to them, marking a significant difference between governments and corporations, that must be considered in detailed comparisons.

4. Oligarchs rise to greatness when they overcome the obstacles that confront them. Therefore, leading citizens are fortunate when competitors plot against them, creating the opportunity of overcoming them and by that struggle to climb higher. For this reason, as a savvy oligarch, when you have the opportunity, you ought to foster some antagonism, so that, having overcome it, your fame will increase.

Reagan appeared so much stronger after surviving John Hinckley's assassination attempt in 1981. Not that Hinckley was put up to the assassination attempt by the FBI, but it had the same effect as if it had been. Immediately after being shot, Reagan's program of tax abatement for the rich that had been widely rejected by the voters and Congress was able to pass by one or two votes. Trump elevated himself to the presidency by overcoming overt resistance of the media and mainstream politicians. The very antagonism of the mainstream media elevated Trump's reputation among voters who felt themselves ignored by neoliberal globalists.

In a related way, the FBI or the police send an agent into a suspected terrorist cell to move it to act when otherwise its members would just talk. When instead they act, the FBI can appear on top of its game by finding the terrorist cell that it itself created from a few disaffected young Muslims doing no more than griping about inequality and prejudice. For example, in the case of the Newburgh Four, the FBI used an informant named Shahed Hussain to sting not only the Newburgh Muslims, but others in Albany and Pittsburgh. Hussain himself was suborned by the FBI to become an informant when he was accused of defrauding immigrants who could not read English.

Corporations and nations should foster a healthy, diverse exchange of ideas, since the higher the stakes, the more corporations benefit from discussion prior to making decisions. Many managers quail at the thought of negotiating differing opinions, and it does require some skill. New ideas often come from diverse populations, while executing plans benefits from agreement about goals and methods.

Leaders who encourage open discussion of diverse opinions end up with stronger governance. This is, however, difficult to prove because the success of Obama's regime as opposed to George W. Bush's regime might be related to factors other than the lack of diversity in the Bush regime. Japanese leaders point out that it is easier to manage a homogenous group during a war or other conflict. Through these examples, we see the various kinds of conflicts and their use or risk to the oligarch.

New media, social media, and enhanced access to representatives through the Internet has actually isolated government officials from their constituents because they are forced to protect themselves from the noise of the populace in order to do their jobs and raise enough money to get re-elected. When combined with laws and regulations that empower people with money, the demise of the major democracies of the world appears increasingly likely. Ironically, while posturing that they preserve freedoms, these conservative rulings will turn out to limit them while empowering oligarchs.

5. New Silicon Valley oligarchs have had better support from loyal employees who worked with them agreeably from the beginning of their ventures rather than those whose ideas about how to develop technology differed. Wozniak, the designer of the Apple computer, rarely conflicted with Jobs. And Gates and Paul Allen worked well together, and their conflicts were productive. But the more open its culture, the larger and more successful a business can become, because it accommodates more diverse talents. Principles of diversity suffer more at the start of a process, when ideas and businesses need to be shielded, than when those ideas and businesses are more resilient and need to grow.

Winning people over often binds them closer than those who are your natural allies or your family. We will simply say that workers who, when first hired, needed a job and assistance to support themselves and their families are won over with the greatest ease. They will serve the oligarch loyally since they want to cancel the bad impression that he formed of them when they were in need: almost everyone wants to appear able to sustain themselves even if their self-reliance remains illusory. Thus, the oligarch extracts more effort from those in need than from those who, serving securely and complacently, may neglect certain responsibilities.

Worker complacency justifies reorganizing companies with some regularity so employees do not feel too secure in their positions and thereby become resentful. The example of IBM's regular reorganizing has been discussed. Several Republican governors in the US have stoked anger among workers who have lost their benefits and pensions to globalization against those who still retain benefits. The governors want workers who were stripped of their benefits to treat those who still have pensions as freeloaders rather than as workers who have paid into the system and negotiated contracts. Usually it is those same governors who presided over the elimination of worker benefits by allowing right-to-work laws to be passed in their states.

In the case of collective farming, even in the rich *chernozem* of the Russian steppes, farmers were not productive because Soviet systems conflicted with the natural cycles that agricultural workers traditionally use to organize their labor. A certain balance between freedom and security seems to satisfy most people, so that when you provide less freedom and more security beyond a certain basic level, people become less productive. When you provide too little security or the media threatens people's confidence, citizens and workers feel vulnerable and assume aggressive attitudes, such as US conservatives who sometimes degenerate into nativist terrorism. Balance supports the oligarchy and the welfare of the people, which is why it remains a key structure in successful states and corporations. In spite of obvious concerns about the disruptive results of revolution, in the longer term, revolution restores balance to the oligarchy when inequality becomes too great. Nevertheless, as history shows, such insurrections signal a change of oligarchs, not the elimination of oligarchic control.

It should come as no surprise that, if only oligarchs are allowed to organize into corporate networks, and workers are forced to negotiate alone with no collective bargaining capability, corporate leaders become too secure and demanding in their positions. Their behavior appears dissolute and high handed. They lose control of their workers and the support of the people except through threats and fear. Only bullies and passive individuals appreciate such a society. Reciprocity is expected and deserved by people at all levels. All people need community support for success in our endeavors, since individuals do not thrive alone.

In developed countries, complacency in the highest ranks of the oligarchy has lost them support of the people. Both Bush II and Trump gained the US presidency while losing the popular vote. The Brexit vote, the rise of populism in France and the US, and resistance to immigration shows the state is losing the support of citizens. Workers in these situations only stay on to do as little as possible, except under a culture of fear applied by the media and in the workplace. These matters must be guided subtly by the hands of responsible groups if they would govern major corporations and countries. Too much direct power must not be allowed to reside either with corporate management or with the workers. Each should feel fairly treated and motivated to do their best.

Since this theme demands it, we advise any oligarch, who by means of secret favors acquires a company, to consider why anyone offered this prerogative. If it was not done through natural affiliation such as family, which is the initial source of the strongest oligarchies, or for an obvious advantage to the benefactors, then you will only keep your backers friendly with great difficulty. It will be impossible to satisfy them, and the individual oligarch will have to take more and greater risks to retain power.

This situation has been the case with the investment banks since the Great Recession of 2007, although the risks for financial firms have been mitigated by the Federal Reserve Bank. To support the banking system, the Fed lowered the overnight lending rate to 0.25 percent so that instead of taking more risk, the carry trade could provide the bankrupt financial institutions with cash until such time as they could manage their own affairs. But this practice did not work as expected because these companies and their executives now feel entitled to such favoritism. In this way, the financial oligarchy preserves itself, but becomes arrogant and vulnerable, a moral hazard for oligarchs.

In the case of the 2007 financial crisis, the general consent of the governed was eroded, and people were easily led to blame government while the true cause was that financial corporations had corrupted government processes. Convincing the people that central government is the cause of their problems has been a key strategy for the most conservative factions of the business community, since, as we have said, smaller units of government are easier and cheaper to control.

Oligarchic wealth does not trickle down to workers. The wealth of oligarchs must be given overtly through taxes, salary increases, and stable benefits packages to keep economies growing. Otherwise, supporting only one class and suppressing scientific progress—another strategy of extreme conservatives—creates a lag in productivity as we have seen throughout the developed world. Failure to increase the wealth of workers slows corporate growth, except for the short time when growth can be fostered through increased efficiency. Also, increasing efficiency too much is another reason for reduced demand in developed nations, since the culture of efficiency and frugality affects workers' mindset, and they are less apt to open their wallets at the store. Any system that runs with very small tolerances creates friction that decreases its effective life. This response to stress is true both physically in machines and psychologically in people.

6. It has been customary for oligarchs, in order to control their companies and countries more securely, to appear both firm in their strategies and open to other points of view, because as everybody knows, nobody has a patent on being correct. Although a strong father figure like Trump appeals to many, an oligarch's span of authority is so broad that you must on some subjects listen to the opinions of specialists and share responsibilities with others.

The impression of being free of external influences makes an oligarch appear as an objective authority able to represent the entire organization. Such a resolute posture acts like a fortress defending against those who plot to work against you and as a refuge from a surprise attacks on your assets and your network. Such dual agency, while practical, may also be undermined and become counterproductive when the authority of the organization that represents that security, like a bank in default, becomes associated with bad behavior, and public opinion threatens the state or the firm's products.

In this way, the lack of resolution of the US Congress in the face of the renewal of the Patriot Act in 2015 was preferable to an authoritative and cohesive position that would misinform the people and the press about the oppressive intentions of the security state. It doesn't matter whether the irresolute behavior resulted from a genuine conflict of interest or was merely passing the buck. The authority of the network, appearing to come from many points of view, reassures some and threatens others.

In another example, the Republican replacement for Obamacare allows the single ideology of small government to prevent the delivery of quality health care to citizens. The fact that who delivers health care is less important than that people are healthy and have access to medical treatment seems to be lost in the urge to ensure that external influences to the health care system, that is, those seeking local control, control the delivery of health care to citizens. The false claim that people are always better served by local agendas and politicians has reduced the health and productivity of US citizens, making them less healthy than those of other industrialized nations with lower life expectancy, higher incidence of lost work days, and greater infant mortality.

Fortresses, either literal or figurative, are useful in specific circumstances. If they are good in one way, they injure you in another. If you have more to fear from your people than from outsiders, then build fortresses, as the Western powers did after WWII to repress the resurgence of the Germans and other Axis nations. But if you have more to fear from outsiders than from the people, you ought to avoid authoritarian saber rattling and focus on strategies like containment, as in the case of Allied policy toward the Soviet Union, agile strike forces to fight insurgents and respond to unpredictable attacks, detailed negotiation as in the Iranian nuclear deal, and effective plans to resist outside threats, as in the case of US corporations facing Japanese and then Chinese incursions into their markets. Such diverse solutions make sense. Different kinds of power control different kinds of territories, wielded by oligarchs in different positions, some more isolated and some transparently in tandem with others. Of course, this is the opposite of common wisdom. And one of the reasons for writing to you is to make visible the actual rather than the advertised strategies of oligarchs.

Individuals protect themselves and their organisms as the permeable fortress of human life. Any organism defends itself first and foremost. In the same way people protect their ideas about the world and their networks. Hence, we make a big deal about altruism, since it is contrary to most normal biological processes that guard each organism and the popular notion of social Darwinism. Yet altruism is so widespread that it must have a strong biological basis in the group, rather than just the individual. The genetic basis of altruism, in the theory of multilevel selection, is endemic to the oligarch's survival mechanism.

The wise oligarch attends to both group and individual needs and carefully balances them. It would have been prudent, for example, if the US government had avoided the hatred of many peoples by not building relationships with them under false pretenses and not supporting dictatorial regimes as the solution to security in post-colonial regions. This is the way Snowden, Assange, and other traitors to the oligarchy view freedom in the West. All these things considered then, we praise both those who design security states and build fortresses, as well as those who promote trade depending on circumstances. The people will in the end resist whoever, trusting in walls, cares little about being hated by the people.

7: Regarding Good Offices

CHAPTER XXI: HOW AN OLIGARCH SHOULD CONDUCT
HIMSELF IN ORDER TO GAIN RENOWN

Nothing makes an oligarch more esteemed than great enterprises. The pyramids of Egypt were built by the slaves of leading citizens to honor Pharaoh. Caesar's victories were backed by his army, a rising equestrian class, many from the senate, and a corps of military engineers, hardly a one-man show. The great construction projects of the past 100 years from the Golden Gate Bridge to the Three Gorges Dam to the moon walks, all galvanized the attention of other oligarchs, their supporting professionals, and people who needed jobs. We have in our time your respected self, founder and CEO of Tesla, Solar City, SpaceX and other ventures aspiring to clean energy and jobs, and by enabling diverse sources to feed the power grid, an oligarchic metaphor itself. How would you do all that alone?

While you support free markets, you also support a carbon tax to control emissions rather than the subsidies Tesla received. Such apparent inconsistencies in an oligarch's policies are irrelevant to your reputation in the long run. In this case, your view on carbon reflects your evolving understanding in your field of expertise.

Although journalists and editors like to make a big deal of apparent inconsistencies, inconsistency is probably more important in grammar and even there questionable in the light of the diverse identities and voices that make up a literate society. In the short run, apparent inconsistencies undermine a leader's effectiveness and support, because people judge him based on their own moral codes that usually rely on consistency to appear believable. Nevertheless, dynamic systems require constant repositioning.

An oligarch sets an example in an organization's internal affairs to nurture social and personal responsibility. Otherwise, people feel they can break the law with impunity, which is the risk to the state of Trump's self-dealing bravado. An oligarch wants workers to feel responsible to finish the job instead of quitting as soon as it is no longer in their self-interest to work for low wages or under conditions contrary to their self-interest. An oligarch's exemplary, didactic behavior is relevant, not only to the workers, but also to structures established for the leadership team, those professionals whose analytic skills may undermine or support your control when you appear inconsistent or make mistakes.

Inversely, Obama was intelligent, a good family man, devout in his religion, and dedicated to his office, but his own leadership team continually contradicted these values in the way it prioritized politics instead of the socially responsible values that the leader espoused. The administration behaved that way to tactically manage Congress and his funders. But those same contradictions overwhelmed his efforts to establish a set of values for the nation and gave more credence to the antisocial conservatives who opposed him in Congress, in boardrooms, and in the blogosphere.

Most professionals claim quite correctly that they can act privately in ways will not affect their professional objectivity or competence; they can compartmentalize. This is true, but the moral codes of the public and the corporate media oversimplify and frequently contradictory the realities of accomplishing things. And it is a very different problem for a French Prime Minister to be caught in an extramarital affair than for a US president. Therefore, a leader must appear to be consistent, even regarding small-minded things that may interfere with great achievements.

The rule that, as an oligarch, you end up eating what you feed your people extends from technology companies to states like Singapore and Dubai. When ghetto dwellers starve, the 0.1 percent may eat caviar, but their forced smiles reveal they may be tasting Spam. Nevertheless, in the future, Obama and Trump, Xi and Putin, Narendra Modi and Merkel will be judged less by their personal behavior and more by their deeds. To gain adherents and win renown, an oligarch must focus first on goals, challenges, and achievements, then on the value of logic, facts, morals, and loyalty that education, corporate media, and religion promote to the people as the primary values of society.

Chapter XXI: How an Oligarch Should Conduct Himself in Order to... 123

An oligarch is respected when you are either a true supporter or a downright enemy, because people want to be clearly affirmed or denied. They seek cognitive closure. The complex realities of diverse effects and ambivalence, or as our forefathers said, mixed blessings, are more difficult to think about, accept, and act upon.

Complexity is manifested in all kinds of disputes. There remains a delicate, conditional equilibrium, for example, between freedom of speech and socially responsible speech. A balanced approach avoids satirizing the poor, the weak, and the oppressed, and yet does not spare leadership, because leaders serve the people and not only themselves. There are many cohorts of binary thinking, but few write or speak effectively about the policies and distinctions connecting the many more than two perspectives of our complex world. A conditional view of free speech relegates that freedom to the public and institutional spheres while responsible speech is appropriate when addressing individuals to avoid insults and injury.

Some espouse spontaneity of speech in isolated circumstances such as creative work, but impulsive speech must include taking responsibility for the effects of what you say. Spontaneity and planning are relevant each to their own spheres and can be simultaneously executed. One cannot manage a multinational corporation spontaneously, yet C-level leaders are often called on to render split-second decisions. To make them, they are trained by years of planning, but when the time comes, they fall back on their technique to deliver that spontaneous decision and the timely phrase.

Today's national governments and major corporations develop points of view regarding moral conflicts to avoid offending people. An oligarch supports equal economic opportunity, women's right to control their own bodies, and the reach of governance in ways that preserve civility and general consent to be governed. Such hedged positions, while keeping the peace, remain one of the main causes of disaffection with governments in the EU and North America, since they are not morally consistent or clearly defined. This is true for both Obama and Merkel, for both Tim Cook and Jack Ma, because corporate media identify many conflicts in binary terms to generate an emotional response from consumers and thereby gain their adherence. Politicians support these false dichotomies to get votes. Thus, the public statements of the press and politicians are often at odds with more nuanced corporate and government negotiations.

Voters and consumers remember being praised or chided for their actions when they were children. That model of behavior plays out in both political and commercial interactions daily as they demand that issues be described as clear conflicts that they can identify with in order to achieve cognitive closure. Without a defined position, many people's attention wanders. It is difficult to generate emotional involvement in politics and commerce without triggering childhood models of discipline and desire. This condition is true for consumer societies and poorer countries.

Politicians and journalists continue to galvanize the attention of the majority by speaking about complex situations in ways that render the tangible issues practically illegible. Nevertheless, they inspire love and hate, because the issues are framed in these clear and simplified arguments. While issues of governance are publicly addressed as binaries, leaders must act with respect to complex, multilevel core uncertainty to assure inclusion of the diverse interests that support their organizations. In resolving this operational difficulty, an oligarch must to avoid overusing the easy path of control by factionalizing issues and populations associated with their networks. Trump, for a defined period, and his advisor, Steve Bannon, however long he keeps the stage, seek to gain control by creating factions among voters and even within their own party, assuming that competition brings out the best in people. Factions have uses, as already discussed, but they are not the appropriate method for all questions of control and governance, especially in important matters requiring general consent like war or climate change.

In order to win an election, governing oligarchs like Trump and Putin today and Silvio Berlusconi and Mustafa Kemal Atatürk in the past have to appeal to many constituencies on many issues. Being definitive on substantive concerns like financial controls or the cloud of war, which may have been precipitated by policy errors, by external considerations like enemy actions, by climate change, or by all of the above, risks resistance from many directions. Taking a strong position on the emotional issues of the day comes easy because those concerns have been predefined and cohorts gathered on either side in ranks like so many soldiers waiting to become cannon fodder.

Even actual binary interactions are complex. If two powerful corporations, like Apple and Samsung, litigate over patents, you only have to fear the winner if your software doesn't operate on its platforms. But if you have been wise in architecting your app on both platforms, you have nothing to fear. If you operate on only one platform, it will always be more advantageous for you to declare yourself and to ally yourself strenuously. In the first case, where your software doesn't operate on both platforms, if you do not declare yourself, you will fall prey to the winner, in this example Apple, to the pleasure and satisfaction of Samsung, which was bested in the initial suits between the two firms. You will have no reasons to offer or anything to protect you when one of them determines whether to use your equipment in the next generation smartphone. The winner does not want doubtful friends who will not support him in court. The loser will not harbor you, because you did not willingly, affidavit in hand, court him.

In other kinds of conflicts, many ethicists insist like Elie Wiesel that "we must take sides." And further that "Neutrality helps the oppressor, never the victim." But among oligarchs an aggressor is not always the most powerful, as in the case of Islamic State. The one attacked is not always blameless in a dispute, civil disobedience being a prime example. So, ethics rarely makes a definitive basis for action, although it often does for publicity purposes like Clinton's appeal for national support for war in the former Yugoslavia. Avoiding the spread of hostilities from Yugoslavia to the rest of Europe was the strategic reason. Rather it is usually more practical to assess your position in any dispute from both long- and short-term views, and then carefully take sides or, if possible, avoid taking sides in order to retain access to both sets of adherents.

Taking sides risks that you may be wrong and suffer for it. Also, in any conflict you may gain some benefits and incur some losses, no matter who wins or who loses. For this reason, quantification of gains and losses, even on moral issues, benefits an oligarch, and most people's minds automatically work that way, although such an approach should only confirm a direction, not be the deciding factor. On the other hand, an oligarch's interests are not served by speaking about the quantification of moral issues, since it arouses anger in many parties. In that case, an oligarch appears to be allowing quantification to lead regarding issues that people want to reserve for what is called deeper understanding.

Oligarchs must recognize that conflicts among them don't turn out well for their networks, as Piketty pointed out. This is a lesson in finance and irony to all who insist that conflict strengthens both leaders and citizens by preserving their prerogatives. History, self-interest, logic, and morality generally support non-violent resolution of conflicts.

The negative outcome of twentieth-century conflicts for many oligarchies also makes clear that either Machiavelli was dead wrong or making a joke of all the petty princes of Europe while pretending to support them. *The Prince* reads like a job application to the Medici who had thrown him in prison when they took over the Florentine Republic. Through his writing, he was eventually hired to write the *History of Florence* in times that were, if possible, even more uncertain than our own. Ambiguity and the expectation of conflict are key drivers of action in *The Prince*. Today, peace and sustainability turn out to be more effective policies than war for preserving the networks of oligarchs. An alternating combination of ambiguity, expectation, peace, and sustainability, and sometimes all four at once, is often operational, there being no fixed rule, only the general assumption that peace smooths the paths of interaction for the oligarch.

An oligarch is thus warned against taking a binary position in planning, even if you take such a position in public. Good results depend more on understanding conditions at the outset, then again at every point reassessed along the way. An oligarch's role in an issue helps you to decide which position or combination of positions to take. Therefore, to gain renown, an oligarch must make clear public distinctions, such as regarding the form of governance, while operating in a nuanced manner at many levels.

You must not be silent except in extraordinary situations. Based on the period prior to WWII and after the second war in Iraq, we agree that silence encourages the tormentor rather than the tormented. So, it appears that oligarchs must sometimes intervene with other oligarchs to maintain a level playing field and a balance of power in both commerce and society. When human lives are endangered, when human dignity is in jeopardy, national borders and sensitivities become less relevant, because the binaries become more operationally true through the channels that form mass opinion. At such times oligarchs are more likely to come into conflict with each other, and this above all must be carefully managed. The issues mentioned around the fragmentation of Yugoslavia are a good case supporting this point, since many forces were in play. The current Middle East conflicts of interests among Turkish, Arab, Iranian, Slavic, Israeli, North American, and European peoples all vying for supremacy, cannot be resolved by morality, but require balancing many points of view and compromises by all.

Wherever men and women are persecuted because of their race, gender, religion, or political views, that place, at that moment, becomes the center of our universe in the same way that any pain in our bodies makes it difficult to go about our daily activities. Chronic pain is the exception. Hence continuous, low-level conflict may be the exception to the axiom stated above. With tolerable pain levels, we compensate and build a culture of endurance like Jewish culture prior to the creation of the state of Israel and African-American culture during slavery, the period of Jim Crow laws, and in the current danger zones for people of color.

In a global society, almost all people end up being subordinated to an oligarch at one level or several. Even oligarchs themselves are absorbed by the false idea of freedom. While leaders are seen to exploit, they are also exploited by the system of production and consumption. The weight of surplus presses all as much as surplus sustains the people in times of want. Oligarchs pursue wealth as consumers with the same energy that the poor seek sales items to feed their families. Oligarchs gain renown both when they achieve a great victory or go against the grain of contemporary assumptions.

Energy leadership pollutes the very air they breathe, requiring a level of denial similar to the low pain levels that induce cultures of endurance. Supporting Israel or Palestine, supporting Saudi Arabia or Iran, supporting India or Pakistan, supporting China or Japan in the dispute over some virtually meaningless islands, supporting freedom of speech or sensitivity in descriptions of the oppressed depend far more on your condition and role than on any intrinsic value associated with those false binaries that manage public opinion and solidify oligarchic power around forms of emotion, forms of government, or forms of behavior that obscure the operational and functional sources of power.

Oligarchs retain power under the disciplinary lash themselves, so there is rarely, as anthropologists say, a big man at the top as there is in isolated clans; instead, there is really only a series of individuals and groups aligning and realigning themselves into social units of shared interests and attitudes about their work, identities, and connections. Those who see Trump and Putin as autocrats miss the point that their network puts them forward to galvanize the attention of the people and manage expectations. Neither Trump nor Putin actually controls operations. As a smart, tough leader, Putin enables other oligarchs so long as they support his financial dealings and posture in the press. Trump so aspires. In this way, the oligarchic network outlasts forms of government that change with technologies and wars.

In business competition, low-level conflict, and other dynamic situations, he who is not your friend will demand your neutrality, while your friend will encourage you to declare yourself with loyalty, arms, and financial support. Irresolute oligarchs, to avoid present dangers, generally follow the neutral path thinking that they may get business or support from whomever is the winner, because what they have to offer has intrinsic value. Sadly, other than readiness and flexibility, no rule can accommodate enough of the cases. Such is the nature of social, political, and environmental interaction. Yet people continue to seek rule-based politics, economics, and culture to reduce the energy required to conduct those activities. A wise oligarch knows that working with your supporters, strongly defending your network, and continually realigning your assets and alliances clear your path to success.

When you declare yourself gallantly supporting one side of a conflict, if your ally wins the case or the war, the victor is not indebted to you forever. Saddam Hussein found this out supporting the US against Iran in the Iran-Iraq war. When he wanted to stop Kuwait from cheating on OPEC's agreed production limits, the bond of amity with the US was destroyed, because humanity is a monument to uncertainty and ingratitude. By oppressing its former ally when he attacked another within the network, rather than seeking a negotiated settlement, the US preferred to engage its war machines and capitalize on Saddam's mistake. The concept of oligarchic loyalty is as foreign today as at any other time. Our global situation is so complex that any oligarch has to subtly manage elusive alliances to stay in office as Merkel has learned.

Victories, after all, are never so complete that the victor must not show some regard, especially to justice. Justice remains one of the most powerful prejudices for humans because it supports individual and social biases toward fairness and self-interest; also, institutions around the world support it.

Even with justice, complexity reigns. If your ally loses, as Austria to Germany in WWII, you may be sheltered for a while, but not forever. While your ally is able, it may aid you. You thereby become companions in fortune that may rise again. In this case, even when the Axis lost the war, the Allies did not further punish the Austrian or German oligarchs, but rather aided them with the Marshall Plan, because it was in the interest of the Allied oligarchs to have strong organizations facing the Iron Curtain. Austria received $468 million from the Marshall Plan while Germany was given $1.4 billion. It is clear how much Austria benefited, since it received 25 percent of the funding of Germany, although its population was only 10 percent of Germany's. In this example, alliance with the losing side was not as problematic as being the instigator of the conflict. Oligarchs are thereby encouraged to choose sides, but not initiate conflict.

When it is not clear who will win a struggle, the oligarch should view it as a lose/lose situation and work to avoid conflict. With so many assassinations of unarmed black men by police throughout the US, a prudent leader at the national level must ally with the coalition that will reduce conflict. In this way, that leader may undermine overzealous policing with the aid of people of color, for whom a policy of not walking while black is hardly sustainable, but only through groups that promote greater safety, including the police.

CHAPTER XXI: HOW AN OLIGARCH SHOULD CONDUCT HIMSELF IN ORDER TO... 129

If your business depends on the community, and you deem the police to be less relevant to your success, you may side with communities of color by funding civil suits against the police. If the communities of color win their suit, you depend on their discretion, but often community leaders can't control youthful exuberance. In this way, even the petit bourgeois operate oligarchically, according to common interests. An oligarch usually avoids being at the discretion of the police and security state, hoping to orient them toward protecting property. Leading oligarchs fund the police and army through taxes, as well as backing suits against them.

When you have an alternative, you must make careful choices, since bad decisions can continue to plague you years later. Bill Clinton allied himself with Wall Street in supporting the repeal of Glass–Steagall, positioning himself and his party as destroyers of middle-class prosperity in order to secure donations from financial services companies. From then on, his supporters on the left could always strengthen their negotiating position by pointing to his connection to Wall Street. Coalitions demand continual negotiation as conflicts of interest arise.

The Republicans, too, were able to capitalize on his error in their opposition to Clinton in 2016. The Clinton Global Initiative donates millions to good causes around the world in alliance with globalists who do not prioritize workers' needs. Charitable oligarchs are widely lauded. Even though CGI supports both local communities and globalized oligarchy, Republicans won white working class votes in 2016 by pointing out how Clinton's network had long neglected the interests of these traditional, working-class Democrats who had been key supporters of the New Deal.

Of course, it did not have to turn out this way, because the Clintons had many other ways to repay financial community donors besides removing such a keystone as Glass-Steagall from the regulatory vault. Only years later did it become clear how much the Clintons overpaid for finance industry support. You might call it an investment with extraordinary ROI?

So, it becomes clearer how both sides are manipulated by financial interests and do not complain in public. First, the Democrats repealed Glass-Steagall, and now Republicans may legislate corporate tax relief. These examples reinforce economic determinism, while at the same time emphasize how the connections of a few dominate transactions that affect many, financial and otherwise. The class binary is highlighted, when the details of oligarchic manipulation are exposed, and the palaver of politics falls silent for a moment. To retain control, however, an oligarch breaks the binary by seeking balance within and among the various interest groups that comprise society.

Many oligarchs choose to influence political outcomes while staying out of office. It is too easy to narrowly characterize their actions when they accept public office. But an isolated, rising individual, like Trump, felt he must seek political office to access channels for business opportunities otherwise denied to him. The question for Trump is the same as any oligarch, whether he has inherited wealth like Trump or is a self-made leader like Bezos. Have his efforts to reach high office engaged Russia in a way that will later unseat him as his pigeons come home to roost? History will tell a tale told by the victor.

Never imagine that corporations and governments can choose perfectly safe courses. An oligarch must expect to tread probabilistic paths, because in ordinary affairs you never avoid one problem without running into another. Prudence consists in knowing how to distinguish the character and importance of each problem as it becomes relevant. Again, complex societies are both multifaceted and unpredictable. Neither ideology nor morality can dictate a safe course for long. In this way, human affairs operate like the rest of the biosphere as you have no doubt noticed even though most cultures suppress this similarity, preferring to limit the options available to people by highlighting the unique aspects of human activity. Rationality and choice filter the flow of events through the body politic. Although uncertain, they direct flows toward productivity or stability, especially when short- and long-term interests are at odds.

An oligarch gains renown by showing yourself a patron of ability. You must honor proficiency in every art, because culture shades how people view their surroundings, and you want to control where the light falls. Simultaneously, you should encourage citizens and workers to practice a variety of professions in commerce, science, agriculture, and every other discipline. In this way, citizens and workers are not deterred from increasing their wealth and improving their well-being for fear of appropriation by government and law in the service of leadership. The form of democracy has a better record in this matter than principalities. Entrepreneurs should start businesses without fear of excessive taxes, but be pleased to pay taxes, because it means that they are making money and at the same time supporting the society that made their freedom of action possible. This is not a plea for generosity against self-interest, but to point out that both individual ventures and societies benefit from balance and mutually supportive policies.

CHAPTER XXI: HOW AN OLIGARCH SHOULD CONDUCT HIMSELF IN ORDER TO...

An oligarch ought to reward those who do these things peaceably, because lasting wealth and authority are founded on peace and stability. Yet even in peace there is little certainty, and often in peace, culture can be stultifying if citizens are deluded that they can pre-empt change. Culture needs to encourage change and growth rather than only reassure with beauty or turn people to stone with special effects that give a false impression about what impacts their lives. An oligarch must, as the Red Queen says, keep running to stay in place. Risks to the oligarchy come with these cultural changes, but a prudent oligarch compensates for change and avoids micromanaging.

An oligarch ought to entertain the people in sports arenas, with Teletubbies, YouTubes, and other spectacles at convenient seasons. Since the Internet now provides a significant lever for action against the oligarch, as the Arab Spring proved, an intelligent leader finds ways to spin even the worst press. Any single level of illegal or problematic action can usually be circumvented. One is more likely to lose one's position or at least reputation, as noted in the case of McClendon, when conflicts appear both as a personal weakness and a failure in the business of your organization.

Every city and rural place in the US is divided into gerrymandered voting districts and neighborhoods that tend toward common culture. Globally, people are organized into societies and their subdivisions. Jurisdictions are diverse, but similar under similar circumstances like mountains and plains, city and rural, dry and fertile, as Alexander von Humboldt pointed out in his botanical investigations. Through these jurisdictions, organizations, and geographies, the oligarch channels populations and promotes ideas.

Technology oligarchs have in recent years sought to undermine these cultures, districts, and neighborhoods to achieve direct access to consumers without relying on intermediary institutions. Social media further exacerbate disintermediation by encouraging hypervigilance and fear of institutions, while people's skill at interacting face to face stagnates. Margaret Thatcher, while Prime Minster of the UK, shocked thoughtful leaders saying, "There is no society, only individuals." Such trends should alarm you.

An oligarch ought to hold intermediate organizations in great esteem and associate with them as bases of power. Showing your support, courtesy, and responsiveness toward leaders of intermediate institutions helps maintain a polite distance of rank, which might please you. An oligarch should not seek to compromise a network as a whole or narrow its scope to the Internet in order to gain renown. Otherwise, new oligarchs will replace you.

An oligarch negotiates such an isolated position only when forced by circumstances to realign certain connections, while maintaining the overall structure of economic and political relationships. In this effort, your reputation can always be bolstered through many networks and subnets, which remain the true channels of power as skills and assets are their contents.

Chapter XXII: Concerning the Administrators of Oligarchy

Hiring subordinates, engaging cohorts, and rallying supporters is vital, since an oligarch cannot manage substantial holdings alone. Administrators are useful in proportion to your skill at discrimination. The first opinion we form of an oligarch, and of your understanding, is by observing the men and women you have around you, the places you work or live, and that you know the difference between the things you own and the people who support you. When your officers are capable and loyal, and your offices well-appointed, but not too lavish, you will be considered astute. Analysis shows that you understand value and the difference between a good showing and ostentation.

But when your subordinates cause problems, we cannot form a good opinion of you, for the first error was choosing them or, if they came with the office, of not replacing them. In this way, we question Trump's use of poet William Blake's aphorism, "The road of excess leads to the palace of wisdom." When Trump uses this sentence, he implies that an excess of consumption, an excess of violence, and an excess of control are a wise course of action. But an environmentally aware oligarch, such as yourself, maintains concern for balance and applies appropriate levels of effort and risk to any task.

By comparing Blake's intention to Trump's goal, Trump shows that he is able to imitate sagacity without understanding it. He continues to project total independence, while trying to build a network composed of like-minded oligarchs. He emphasizes his individual excellence in negotiation, strategy, and support for conservative causes without acknowledging that his distinction is projected as much by his administrators and subordinates as by himself. Considering the interdependence of the twenty-first-century Presidency, the fantasy of isolated individual greatness seems all the more absurd. From a related perspective, the helpfulness to the reader, in contrast to the bravado, of the strategy of recycling used to write this book can be

CHAPTER XXII: CONCERNING THE ADMINISTRATORS OF OLIGARCHY   133

judged by whether it effectively links the forms of states and corporations to the operations of governance, so that readers recognize their ecology.

As distinguished from Trump, Sandy Weill, Citigroup CEO, was considered clever not only for his achievements but also for his use of Jamie Dimon as his detail man. As derived from Machiavelli, you can discriminate among three classes of intellects: one which comprehends by itself and can act to maintain and enhance the prerogatives of leadership while improving customer satisfaction and growing relevant numbers. Another appreciates what others comprehend and can implement another's initiative, but may or may not be able to understand the difference between oligarchic prerogatives and attracting new business or enhancing wallet-share. The third neither comprehends himself nor relevant examples and frequently indulges in frivolous pursuits and shows of excess. Dimon was in the first category because, later, when internal politics forced him out of Citi, he became head of JP Morgan Chase, at the time the leading bank in the world.

Many bankrupt oligarchs fail to understand the responsibilities of leadership and only seek to line their pockets and deliver graft to their friends and families, which they do for a time, but are soon reduced to a dismal state. China's General Xu Caihou, in the "cash for rank" scandal, and Ling Jihua, on many charges of corruption, were good examples of oligarchs who chose administrators for the wrong reasons. In his first administration, Obama hired several secretaries based on their political affiliations rather than on their skills, arousing resentment both in Republican and Democratic circles.

To form an opinion of a potential subordinates, there is one test which never fails. When you notice that the candidate thinks too often of personal interests, such an individual will never make a good subordinate. You know this from the candidate's sentence structure, posture, and answers to questions about conflict of interest. Applying theory of mind to understanding subordinates, and peers for that matter, pays off.

In this matter, there is no better example than Cheney's vice presidency. He was put forward by his party not merely as a vice president, but as policy implementer and coordinator of a conservative Republican faction led by the oil patch and arms manufacturers. In the business of the state, Cheney compromised Bush as president as if Iago were vice president. If we did not understand how the subordinate was actually running the show for his own benefit, or in the parlance of the time, the tail was wagging the dog, then the whole administration seemed a mystery. In the end, with venal subordinates and secret agendas, Bush II's administration incurred multiple disasters both military and financial.

As a result, people began to fear that the US was an unreliable ally and its reputation was compromised. Obama sought to right the ship. To some extent he succeeded, although not without many errors due to his inexperience and the lack of experienced, devoted secretaries early on who were selfless in serving the people. Rather, in his first term, political operatives served their constituencies from their cabinet positions. Under Trump, the situation has worsened with family members assuming official advisory positions. Trump's primary advisors do not act as if they had the well-being of the people or the integrity of the state in mind. Rather, the Trump administration promotes family and corporate interests as you would expect in a ruling oligarchy.

To keep subordinates honest, an oligarch ought to study, respect, and empower them, sharing both awards and cares. An oligarch must show by example that subordinates cannot stand alone, but need the network to make the state, the company, and the intellectual fabric work effectively. Honors should not make them desire more and think themselves independent. Personal wealth should not make them think themselves superior.

Difficult situations should not make them dread inevitable changes. The subordinate must understand and foresee change, acting before it becomes an emergency, but not too soon, that is, before it is certain in what direction the change will go. When the future is uncertain, which is most of the time, plans should be drawn with alternative scenarios. With such an approach, the US would not have gone into the second Iraq war without a plan for rebuilding and maintaining the state after the fall of Saddam Hussein. When subordinates and oligarchs toward subordinates are so disposed, they can trust each other, but when it is otherwise, the end will always be disastrous for either one or the other or both and thus for the nation, the company, and the theory.

The same is not true of the face-men of the oligarch who operate a civil government. Many oligarchs want to run their businesses and not be bothered by the added compromises required by state governance. Such oligarchs must support the political campaigns of several officials who agree with them in principle and even those who don't agree with them in order to retain access to the channels of power. These financial arrangements range from direct contributions, to support for campaigns, and to donations to charities. Less care may be taken about politicians to whom you donate, since you will be only one of several that the official represents. But when your choice proves to have been obviously faulty, then oligarchs together should work to reroute the network without such alterations being transparent.

The virtues that you as an oligarch value must be sought in people that act on your behalf in government, except that you cannot be seen to be the sole funder of a candidate's election. Hence every government official supporting the oligarchy, and there are very few who don't, must be able to juggle the points of view of several oligarchic interests. Under these conditions, which are structurally fairly constant while specific connections are dynamic, the network supports the power of individuals. The network infrastructure refers here to the business connections, institutional interactions, and family ties of the oligarch. Across that network run the flows of funds, interests in specific programs such as construction projects or tax reform, and information about laws, culture, and appropriate positions on the issues of the day.

Representatives of oligarchs should where possible avoid having personal interests in locations where conflict often occurs, like the state of Israel, the Middle East, and Russia, unless the oligarch needs change in one of those jurisdictions. Otherwise the politician must be very talented, such as New York Senator Charles Schumer who is able to support Israel and Wall Street, while retaining his reputation as a liberal politician in spite of these obvious allegiances to conservative networks. Such talented representatives of oligarchy are few, but the US Congress has more than one of them.

As an oligarch, you must not be envious of your political supporters' other funders, understanding that even in an oligarchy as obvious as the US, multiple interests must always be accommodated, because the country is so large, complex, and wealthy, with many different oligarchs and subnets. It is in fact the common network structure of all organizations that makes it possible for such differences, even important ones, to exist side by side in the mind of individual leaders and the operations of the state and corporation. Consistent administration, with flexible rules, is an inherent, by which we mean natural, process and not a form of policy.

Chapter XXIII: How Flatterers Should Be Avoided

We must not leave out an important influence on oligarchy, a danger that an oligarch avoids with difficulty unless you are careful and discriminating. The offices of government, business, education, and medicine are full of yes-men and lobbyists who hope to manipulate leadership to their own advantage.

They easily succeed, since most people are so complacent, so involved with their own ways of thinking, so engaged with illusions about their unique position that the thoughts and motivations of others seem opaque.

On the other hand, most five-year-old children learn that others may think differently than they do. They have developed a theory of mind. An oligarch who cannot effectively engage theory of mind often loses control of an organization or is forced to adopt tyrannical methods. The individual and culture that ignore theory of mind lose the ability to understand the causes and consequences of others' actions. Such a culture ultimately assumes that you cannot understand another person's situation. Consumer culture, obsessed with individual desire and uniqueness, largely denies that the thoughts of others are accessible. As a result, consumers are easily manipulated.

This species of blindness is sometimes the case with powerful individuals, the wealthy, and romantic or narcissistic creators and inventors. The savvy oligarch sees into the minds of others, even when some of them may exhibit symptoms of consumerism and sociopathology. The notion that we cannot speak for others or understand their positions turns out to be true only for those who fail to develop a robust theory of mind and learn to use it in practical affairs.

Of course, we cannot fully feel another person's pain or know their situation, and so should defer to what people say about themselves most of the time. But when complex or critical decisions need to be made, the discerning oligarch understands the motivations of advisors. Some lobbyists learn to speak for others as a way to express their own desires. Such presumptuous behavior alienates those who seek self-determination, but attracts those seeking easy solutions to complex problems. Therefore, the oligarch must learn to use theory of mind carefully, since in conflicts among oligarchs, those who can see into the minds of their adversaries usually come out on top. Lobbyists and yes-men cannot easily manipulate an oligarch with a well-developed theory of mind.

Oligarchs deeply absorbed with their own affairs and methods, who believe their own logic, and who do not lift their heads to see others around them, are vulnerable to those who use the very tactics of oligarchic deception to mislead them. Oligarchs defending their positions too vigorously and only seeking sympathetic subordinates run the danger of incurring the contempt of their employees, citizens, and peers. The best way to protect yourself from yes-men and lobbyists is to let people know that the truth does not offend you.

In all related affairs, the entire context of the matter must be known and understood for an effective decision to be reached. Trump spent hours in briefing rooms before bombing a Syrian military base. Obama listened carefully before sending SEAL Teams to take out Osama bin Laden. But if everyone is permitted tell you the truth, respect for you diminishes because it appears that you do not have your own opinion and cannot chart a steady course. So, it is up to you to understand that when people give you great detail on only one side of an issue in order to gain your adherence for their schemes and to make you complacent by telling you what you want to hear, you should remember that you are using these same tactics on your citizens, employees, and other oligarchs to control your domains.

To minimize these risks, an oligarch can embrace a third course by choosing specialists in specific disciplines as well as environmentalists who can put diverse ideas together to analyze problems from several points of view. These thought leaders should not be bought or allowed to buy you, but should come from the universities of your province or locality and independent think tanks (a difficult task given today's private funding of them in support of partisan interests), rather than from corporations with their own interest in mind, because local and affiliated specialists are more likely to have common cause with you. That said, you must also acquaint yourself with points of view that you do not agree with, because they often contain significant value that should not be overlooked. How many legislators, for example, now wish they had more carefully considered the truth behind the administration's claims about Saddam Hussein's weapons of mass destruction before supporting the war in Iraq.

Your advisors should be encouraged to speak the truth. But when they differ from your positions, your subordinates should tell you their opinions only in the correct context. In planning and decision-making meetings, advisors should be allowed to fully voice their points of view. You should not allow a glib speaker to dominate, but rather hear all perspectives, since often one point of view makes sense at the beginning, but by the end of the discussion, you realize that you need to support another position. In a situation where you are about to make a costly mistake that you do not see, your subordinate should ask you to step out of the meeting for a moment, and there, out of earshot, make the point and give you a moment to digest it before returning to the meeting. Then the subordinate should speak only on the relevant topic.

An oligarch ought to question advisors about everything and listen to their opinions, but afterward form independent conclusions. With these counselors, either separately and collectively, conduct yourself so that each knows that the more freely they speak, the more they are appreciated. Beyond these meetings, pursue your purposes resolutely, because often making a decision, even an imperfect one, is a better course than vacillating, especially when resources are massed for a major initiative. This is true because, although there may be key individual decisions, the impact of many decisions in a large initiative usually overwhelms any individual decision. As is often heard, the perfect is the enemy of the good; this is true because of the complexity of most interactions. Unless you hear multiple points of view and yet make independent decisions, an oligarch is driven by disguised interests, overthrown by yes-men, and is so often twisted around by varying opinions that subordinates become contemptuous. The press will quickly exploit that situation.

We know intuitively that bribery and lobbying are related. There are reams of academic papers that try to draw the line between legitimate issue advocacy and corruption. This problem is crucial, since both democracies and autocracies need advocates in government to represent the points of view of varied constituencies. Yet once a problem is presented to an official, equality of opportunity, one of the hallmarks of well-being, is compromised if special interests continue to be the only parties consulted for the solution. Often a minority deserves special attention because, for example, so many people are concerned about issues like allergies to food or the impact of water use in dry climates—it can be a life-and-death matter where all sides need to be heard. Michigan governor Rick Snyder failed his citizens by listening only to those who wanted to save money, ignoring the fact that the lead pipes delivering Flint's water were poisoning the people. Saving money is important; poisoning your own citizens should be avoided.

Looked at this way, it becomes clear again that the forms of state and corporate governance fail to explain the full breadth of concerns around complex issues, yet citizens and employees can usually only access governance through the form as provided to them. Thus, the oligarchy, that is the operational, situational level of governance, is uniquely suited both to solve the problems and to profit from the solutions. Our brightest minds, however, seem to have difficulty drawing a meaningful distinction between, on the one hand, handing someone an envelope full of cash, flooding a senator's campaign war chest, allowing primarily corporate interests to write trade deals like the Trans-Pacific Partnership, and, on the other hand, hearing all sides of an issue from specialists and affected parties. The case of US v Harriss (1954) is a good example of such equivocation, in which lobbyists have a different status depending on whether they advise members of Congress or its staff. Such hedging about what is considered lobbying strengthens the positions of institutions and weakens both the form and operations of the state and the corporation.

Why this difference seems obscure can only be explained by a preference for subterfuge in operations and those small-scale, controllable interactions that happen behind closed doors. It also speaks to the value of bureaucracy for multinational organizations. Also, an oligarch knows that lobbying is far more effective than bribery, and it's legal. A briber wants to circumvent the law once. A lobbyist wants to write a law so that there may, for example, be no limits to the amount of campaign funding that can come from corporations to candidates, essentially legalizing arms-length bribery.

The Citizens United decision appears as the most destructive decision in recent years by identifying money with speech, a decision that does not pass the sniff test. Clearly, they are not the same, but legal inference has made it appear so. Until this operational link in the network is severed, democracy is an increasingly ineffective form of government, and citizens and workers must focus more closely on influencing operations, if they expect a seat at the table in making decisions that affect them. A wise oligarch handles such situations outside of the form of government, through strong, independent regulatory bodies, because similar conditions of large populations exist everywhere in every form of governance.

Citizens United has made the wealthy too powerful. Conservative money flooded certain Wisconsin, Michigan, Ohio, and Pennsylvania voting districts in the 2016 elections from the coffers of the Koch network of conservatives. The Koch network did not have to support Trump, but only get out voters in the appropriate districts in support of local elections. Trump's victory in those districts and consequently in the national election shows that cut-rate national campaigns supported by large dark pools of money flooding local elections formed a network able to turn Clinton's otherwise unstoppable tide on the national level. These types of operations weaken all classes over time. Citizens United exposes the network of control to hackers of systems at every level such as foreign governments, people of color agitating for safety in their neighborhoods, gender-identified groups seeking civil rights, laborers seeking job security and benefits, mass affluent families seeking tax abatements that are similar to oligarchs, and other groups who had been coopted to defend the 0.1 percent's money. The oligarchic system of control, rendered transparent, requires much more tending and funding to secure it. An oligarch seeking alliances with a broader set of class interests runs government more cheaply and effectively for those wider interests.

Narco states, autocratic states, religious and secular dictatorships, and democracies hollowed out by operational circumventions are oligarchies ruled by graft and corruption, when power and influence are traded in secret. These states operate as oligarchies in that leaders have many advisors controlling parts of their holdings. We have advised that your representatives have both skin in the game and an independent set of interests to be effective rather than the pawns of a dominant principal, as some insecure leaders suppose all legislators, citizens, and workers need to be.

Further, if, as an oligarch, you are too secretive and do not communicate plans within your circle, you cannot receive useful opinions. When you try to put secret plans into effect, and they are revealed, those who operate the government, corporation, religion, school, or gang will obstruct their execution. You will then be required to change your mind because those that must implement your plans will thwart them. So, you must either listen in advance or prepare for chaotic rule, since what you do one day, you undo the next. In this case, no one ever understands what you wish or intend to do, and no one can rely on your solutions. Trump must learn this lesson in office, since he did not learn it in business.

As an oligarch, therefore, you ought always to take counsel prior to acting, but only when you wish and not when others wish, except in emergencies when you should in any case receive counsel. Sometimes emergencies are hard to recognize among the stresses of leadership when so many important matters bear on each moment. Thus, an oligarch should rather generally discourage advice out of context. You ought, however, to be a constant inquirer and then a patient listener concerning your inquiries. When you learn that any one, on any issue, has not told the truth, you should be noticeably angry.

Some people think that an oligarch's good judgement emanates solely from advisers. This point of view fails to acknowledge the oligarch's skills. These people deceive themselves in order to cover up their own insecurity. Many oligarchs gain power and control in the first place because they are skilled at navigating through diverse and often contradictory information to reach an effective action. An impractical oligarch will never take good advice and a skilled oligarch distinguishes among different points of view.

CHAPTER XXIII: HOW FLATTERERS SHOULD BE AVOIDED

An effective leader will take advice from experts, but when they disagree, as pointed out, must still be prepared to make a decision.

Good advisors, those with a track record of success, strengthen you. For example, those Republican leaders who listened to James Baker's advice on foreign affairs benefited, and those Democratic leaders who paid attention to Richard Holbrooke when he negotiated the Bosnian settlement were happily surprised. Sadly, Holbrooke failed to convince Obama to avoid sending additional troops to Afghanistan, and the US was forced to withdraw without any additional advantage. Now Trump, having ceded control of defense to James Mattis, runs the risk of allowing the military to overly influence the political sphere. Perfection is not achievable, but you can approach the best solutions with the best people. We repeat that large organizations implement many poor decisions, but are not destroyed when the majority of decisions support oligarchic intent more than the single mistake. You do not need to seek perfection or perfect correctness even in idealism, because such rightness and the heights of efficiency are not sustainable; they make the person and the system brittle.

The Holbrooke example shows how an oligarch who is not experienced, as in the case of Obama, should take great care in receiving advice from more than one advisor on one subject. In team decision-making, you must be a strong and decisive leader. The reason for this axiom is that you will never get united counsel. You will not know how to unite them unless you yourself are an expert in that issue. Counsellors will think of their own interests, and the leader will not know how to control them or to see through them. Your advisors cannot behave otherwise, because people will always prove untrue to you unless they are kept honest by constraint or through careful management of their self-interest as in the case of Tito's Yugoslavia.

This is especially true in the world of financialized politics in the US where oligarchs have made the mistake of allowing their power to become visible, instead of unclear as it had been before. As a result, intelligent people are driven to focus on their own financial interest, disrupting the nation. The net effect of many individual, conflicting interests is not stability, but chaotic and unpredictable vacillation. These problems are only just beginning and may result in far more autocratic regimes than US citizens are accustomed to. If self-interest is made the common operational principle of government, NGOs, and corporations, the oligarchy will lack cohesive intent.

For example, Jack Quinn, an excellent Democratic advisor, is now running his own consultancy with ex-Senator Tom DeLay, a convicted felon. Both men are working for commercial enterprises, promoting drilling in the Arctic and suppressing healthier school lunches for the benefit of agribusiness. Quinn as a legislator was helpful to the people. Initially, then, while Citizens United appears to support moneyed interests, one may check back in a few years to see whether it has been reversed or whether the US government is operating as an inherited aristocracy, having lost any resemblance to the free society predicted by its Declaration of Independence and the ideals of democracy. What will happen cannot be predicted, but exposing the roots of power is rarely desirable for the oligarch.

An oblivious oligarch may be governed by a skilled and aggressive advisor, but such a counselor will inevitably try to usurp the organization. This happened to Bush as mentioned with Cheney. It happened again when the inexperienced Obama had to give his White House chief of staff, Rahm Emmanuel, control of Chicago to avoid having Emmanuel's aggressive personality eclipse his own. The administration was disrupted when Emmanuel alienated Congress. Chicago was a reward for his service to the party. It must be inferred then that good counsel is a product of the skilled oligarch and advisor together, and not of toadies, sycophants, and minions.

8: On Risk Management and Marketplace Mentality

CHAPTER XXIV: OLIGARCHS WHO HAVE LOST CONTROL
OF THEIR ORGANIZATIONS AND NETWORKS

The previous suggestions, read carefully, will enable a new oligarch to solidify leadership and appropriate connections. Building a reputation is vital since the actions of new oligarchs are more closely watched than those of long-term holders of public office, asset holders, and executives, and they have fewer connections to strengthen their network. When they show that they are capable, they gain more adherents and linkages. They bind allies more tightly and efficiently than old money because people are attracted more by the shiny present opportunity, and older alliances have more baggage and potential resentments that may smolder for years before flaring up. Since a new leader has to establish an organization, and strengthen it with good practices, good arms, good allies, and a good example, it would be a double disgrace to anyone who, born into an oligarchy, loses a position through lack of skills or bad behavior.

Consider those oligarchs who have lost their positions in our times, such as Saddam Hussein, Mubarak, Berlusconi, Eliot Spitzer, McClendon, Kenneth Lay, and many others. More fail than succeed. They share one or more of several defects: failure to communicate bad news which might have gained support from their adherents, personal misbehavior or illegal behavior; failure to understand the points of view of others; listening to flatterers and lobbyists as pointed out earlier; and climbing into a seat of power from warring factions within their organizations. Some incurred employee or citizen hostility through their failure to provide jobs or security. Some leaders were forced into war to avoid internal rebellion, such as Slobodan Milošević in Serbia, or made to merge with a more stable firm, such as Marissa Meyer was made to at Yahoo.

Some oligarchs keep the people friendly, like Carter, but do not know how to gain support from other oligarchs. Some imagine themselves in sole command, like Perón or Trump, when the network is the primary mechanism of control. Far more power is lost to oligarchic peers than through popular insurrection or revolutions, which are notable but rare. Such losses may stem from corporate competition, disruptive technology, or civil war. Lyndon Baines Johnson's Great Society failed to sustain oligarchic wealth, apparently leading to the rise of the conservative insurrection when economic stagnation occurred through a more normal failure of continued growth after WWII. The collapse of the New Deal network appeared to come from disaffection of the people, but actually occurred due to withdrawal of oligarchic support because corporations felt they needed to reduce their obligations to a society that painted an increasingly intolerable picture of their role as leaders.

Carter gained power through grassroots support because the normal path to the presidency, through local party leaders, had been disrupted in the early '70s by democratic reforms to the primary process. He lost control to conservative corporate interests and hadn't had time to fully develop his own network. In the absence of these kinds of defects, states that have power enough to keep an army in the field cannot be easily lost. Leading parties that pay close attention to their donors and companies with little competition and sufficient market control cannot be lost unless technology changes.

Spitzer had an ideal position as an attorney general fighting corruption, but when he became Governor of New York, he was exposed for frequenting prostitutes. His aggressive behavior toward law-breaking oligarchs meant that he had no support from them when his philandering was exposed. He ignored the common ground of all oligarchs that we have spoken of frequently. Since he also had no support from those who disliked his illicit behavior, the combination of illicit behavior and lack of network support forced him from office.

In 2013, Berlusconi, after many scandals involving underage prostitutes, which apparently is not the same kind of concern as it is in the US and many scandals involving tax evasion in his communications empire, fell from power. Over a weekend, Berlusconi threatened to topple the left-right coalition government of Prime Minister Enrico Letta over proposed VAT increases of 1 percent. He raised the stakes by ordering the five Cabinet ministers of his own People of Freedom party to resign from their posts in protest against Prime Minister Letta. These irresponsible moves undermined Letta's efforts to make his country more attractive to financial markets, but weakened Berlusconi's international standing even more. So, it may be said that the oligarchy itself policed Berlusconi when he attacked financial oligarchs who were given benefits by his adversaries, as we saw with Spitzer.

Financial oligarchy isn't the only power in the world, but the international financial community is the only global power that functions with a similar operating model in all developed countries (except for a few Islamic banks), and it closes ranks when that operating model is threatened. Such is not the case among different forms of government or other kinds of corporations like global energy companies that operate more narrowly and variously. We already talked about the European oligarchs closing ranks around Greek debt, further weakening that already devastated state. The operating model of finance cannot appear to make an exception for Greece, because other debtor nations and debtor organizations might follow the its example. Argentina, having its own currency, was in a different condition, and Kirchner could legally continue in office.

Therefore, do not let US oligarchs like Dick Fuld, Jimmy Cayne, Stan O'Neal, and Angelo Mozilo blame others for the loss of their power after the Great Recession. Rather, understand that their losses stemmed from delusions of power. In quiet times, they did not secure their assets and networks, but continued to leverage their assets beyond prudent levels, without taking some money off the table. It is a common human defect not to make any provision in the calm against the tempest or adequately distribute resources to reduce risk. Frequently, decisions under stress are made as if change will only be minimal and similar to recent changes rather than looking at the longer history of volatility. When bad times arrive, weak leaders think only about defending themselves. They hope that the people and their cohorts would support them as Fuld thought. But other oligarchs remember, and the people, while quick to forgive, will not forgive a betrayal of trust.

Nevertheless, time passes, and the corporate media distract the people so that they forget the financial errors of the debt economy. With media support, we see how the combination of Citizens United and technology-shortened memory has put the investor class back in the driver's seat in the

2016 election. Even Trump, who has alienated many oligarchs and is not loved in gilded halls other than his own, represents that investor class, since real-estate wealth depends on loans from the financial industry.

We can see the disingenuous attitude of oligarchs who have not been caught in the collapse, but rather who benefited from it, like Dimon who said, "How do I feel about CEOs who walked away with $150 million and their company blew up? It's outrageous!" And then when he was caught in the six-billion-dollar London Whale trading scandal, called it a "tempest in a teapot." So, it is easy to understand how one speaks differently depending on the situation, and we have discussed conditional truth at length already.

Overall, such losses result from excessive focus on one's personal interests and sociopathic or narcissistic behavior, all of which the sensible oligarch avoids. Environmentally sound business practices extend to all levels of interaction, far beyond simply lowering carbon output. Attention to the many relationships in the biosphere mirrors the connectedness in complex society. Ecology within the oligarchy demands that an individual oligarch recognize when personal behavior prompts change and when the group controls change through the network. This binary exhibits many configurations and goes not only one way or the other; the binary is multi-lateral.

Chapter XXV: What Probability Can Effect in Human Affairs, and How to Manage It

Despite 500 years of scientific research and validation to the contrary, many people still believe that the affairs of the world are governed by deities and that people with their skills in governance cannot effectively direct events. The inertia that religious beliefs induce does not go unnoticed by leaders at many levels. They are encouraged by what they have noticed about human behavior to endorse the idea that it is unnecessary to put concerted effort into our activities, but to let our emotions and their authority govern our labors. This opinion is further promoted by consumer product manufacturers who advertise that customers can enjoy themselves as much as they want, without much effort or experiencing negative consequences from their impulsiveness, certainly an idea that has been repudiated by recent events.

Pondering this situation, we are from time to time inclined to this opinion, because so many outcomes appear arbitrary. We, too, are subject to occasional despair. Nevertheless, we understand that there are interactions among complex events, environmental connections, other people, and ourselves that require continual negotiation. External events affect many of our actions, but often, although not always, we can shape those events. Some situations are more subject to chance or changing external conditions, but even then, a prudent oligarch can remain secure by carefully distributing your assets, although distributing the targets of risk is far more difficult than the usual financial advisor can fathom or admit to understanding. Our mistakes control another portion of our results, while our correct intentions sometimes win the day. A single cause is rare; more likely multiple forces are at work.

For example, why did oil prices crash in 2015? Competition between traditional drillers, shale frackers, oil sands extractors, and deep-water drillers increased supply while lower demand around the world exacerbated the situation. None of the major players wanted to reduce production, which they thought would result in losing market share to those who did not cut production. So, supply reached record levels and prices dropped by 75 percent.

Under these conditions, both Saudi and US participants saw an opportunity to increase the bite of sanctions on Russia, ISIS, and Venezuela, increasing their determination to keep producing even as prices continued to drop. Saudi producers wanted to reduce competition from higher cost US shale oil and so continued to pump. The oil oligarchs were fighting each other instead of collectively managing production, and so their market collapsed. The political vector that pits Islamic against Christian nations further encouraged US-Saudi competition. The nationalist push toward US energy independence added to frackers' ability to gain wider network support for continued production. These events may be an object lesson for any conflict among oligarchs.

Are you still looking for a single cause of the collapse? All producers were also becoming increasingly concerned about renewables like solar and wind energy, which had recently become significantly cheaper. This is especially true because Solar City offered to supply electricity to homes for about the same price as the utility companies that use oil, coal, and nuclear energy do, but with no upfront investment. The threat from renewables had become a serious concern for traditional fuel sources.

Any one of those problems would be insufficient to cut prices so drastically, but together they radically changed the oil and gas market. The notion that there is a single cause cannot be true in these large-scale tidal shifts, any more than any one oligarch completely controls the affairs of states or even those of a large corporation. Complexity rules the oligarchy, and leaders hold their positions by knowing how to deal with intricate situations.

Looked at from another perspective, the thought that your actions are not dependent on the outside world or other people and that objectivity refers only to self-reliance seems absurd. Remind yourself how, in your field of expertise, you are successful in the long run because you spend so much of your time hedging your holdings and bolstering against external threats. Sometimes these threats come from competitors in your field, sometimes from your own shortcomings. Sometimes threats come from causes that are not human such as hurricanes, earthquakes, drought, and disease, sometimes from an apparently arbitrary confluence of events. Whether the risks to your control are human or otherwise, or all of the above, the odds are that all will not go smoothly, and you will have to model your assets and ideas for sustainability. This means that you benefit from building solutions around probabilities and hedging to reduce the volatility of your holdings—be they financial, hard assets, or ideas. Your imagination best operates as one tool among many; it is not a strategy. Diversifying assets is more effective than locking them up together. Multiplying paths to your goals increases the likelihood that you will succeed. Again, diversification really means selecting assets and points of view that are both uncorrelated and inversely correlated. The approach is time-consuming and expensive, but the confidence that all your choices will be correct may not work out as you hope.

Establishing confidence levels for your plans, where projections are understood as probabilistic and operating in ranges of solutions, rather than assuming that a single value can identify risk, has helped corporations, banks, and the state security apparatus. Government officials, on the other hand, because they have to satisfy so many points of view, lose credibility by approximation, since critics doubt governmental policies when they are not exactly in line with strict predictions that gratify voters' heroic self-image as unique. An electorate aware of these differences between authoritative pronouncements and actual events is less likely to vote for leaders' empty promises.

Most electorates do not operate with respect to these principles. Hence, the absence of exacting forecasts helps fatalist critics accuse officials of incompetence when the officials are simply telling it like it is: difficult to predict. As a defense against unreasonable expectations of government performance, Obama made a good point when he said that we need to try many solutions to terrorism before we are sure which policies will be effective. Unfortunately, he was not able to try anything similar to the

Marshall Plan in the Middle East, because the indigenous administrative class was designed to be too weak to implement it, as you will remember from the example of how Britain created Iraq.

For large corporations, prediction is difficult and predictive ranges may be wide. Limiting the methods that you use to calculate success helps to narrow the range of quarterly reports. These quarterly profit and revenue reports emphasize short-term planning. They keep executives in their jobs by narrowing the ranges of predictions because many participants in financial markets want to trade for short-term profit. Success in performing within those ranges must be rewarded and failure criticized. Even when profit surpasses forecasts, management must not reward those surpassing projections by too much lest subordinates sandbag to game the system. It makes sense then, even when you understand probabilistic thinking, to try to perform as predictably as possible, because you know that so much of both external events and internal strife are unpredictable and volatile.

Machiavelli compares fortune to one of those raging rivers, which when in flood overflows the plains, and all yield to its violence. This dramatic image attracts the reader's emotions, but far more frequently, if not more devastating, are failures that could have been prevented with longer term planning and positioning.

Focusing too closely on the possibilities of disaster allocates too many resources to security. Further, the politics of fear makes citizens angry and resistant, reducing the general consent to be governed. Under the regime of fear that appears to dominate political theater in our times, insufficient attention is paid to those activities that can be controlled, such as not putting too many assets in that flood-prone river valley in the first place. The one contrary example that we must pay attention to is the risk of human overproduction to the planet as a whole. Even so, the risks of surplus are manageable with good planning. These plans are necessary because creation of surpluses is one good hedge, as long as those surpluses remain available.

Protecting the target of the risk fails when large-scale disasters strike, as the builders of the Great Wall of China and the Maginot Line discovered. Security measures take attention away from more important plans for distribution of assets and reinforcing the well-being of the people. When security fails, your entire advantage is swept away without hedging and effective distribution. Human nature is such, however, that many oligarchs, when the weather becomes fair, do not provide for hard times, but rather spend freely and declare victory loudly. The politics of hope, however, makes more sense for politicians to apply, as its opposite clearly has not improved our societies.

We have discussed fiascos in corporate pension plans that have both failed to support workers in retirement and garnered resentment from those workers without pensions. These plans have to be re-engineered to prevent companies from bankruptcy and states from insolvency. But the solution is not for oligarchs in business and government to put responsibility on the workers. As pointed out, the more conservative pension plan of Social Security can, with small adjustments, manage the huge US working population for many decades. Oligarchs, who, failing to understand the relative merits of small tax increases compared with loss of trust of the entire population, mistake a small loss for a large loss and try to destroy the social safety net that gives credibility to government, corporations, and other controlling institutions. Yet there are those small-minded oligarchs who fundamentally misunderstand their long-term self-interest and seek chaos in government to avoid its scrutiny of their self-defeating strategies of fear-mongering and banking illicit profits.

If you consider how global corporate management, governments, planners, and lobbyists attend to issues of population growth and climate change, you will understand that these groups continue to be the source of errors in judgement about future prospects. These oligarchs have apparently decided that their short-term self-interest encourages them to appear to do nothing about such issues, while working quietly on them in the background. It is vital to note, however, that revealing the entire truth is far from helpful to the smooth running of oligarchies. In fact, the whole truth is usually impossible to divulge, because of the huge amount of information necessary to describe it. And the people's boredom and short attention span threatens oligarchic power as Hillary Clinton discovered.

Even if organizations are defended by proper methods that take into account the large ranges of probable outcomes of globalization, climate change, and population growth, oligarchs must avoid becoming too isolated by talking only to each other. The global collapse of 2007 resulted from imagining that the financial system was a closed loop. Trump's administration has already exhibited this fatal flaw. This we consider enough to say concerning resistance to fortune in general.

Focusing on the particular, a risk taker may be successful today and ruined tomorrow without any change of strategy or character. This arises from causes that have already been discussed, namely, that an oligarch who relies entirely on fortune and spontaneity and not enough on plans that can be modified according to circumstances suffers when conditions change. You are then as much at risk as if you relied too heavily on plans and not enough on individual initiative. A flexible planner succeeds by directing actions earnestly and forcefully according to the conditions of each situation and in line with the culture of the time, while understanding that plans gang aft a-gley.

Oligarchs act in a way that leads to power, glory, wealth, and personal satisfaction. They get there by various methods—one with caution, another with haste, one by force, another by skill, one by patience, another by its opposite. Each reaches the goal by a different method and usually a combination of methods. Applying what works without risking apparent future harm can easily be the motto of anyone who does not let morality become the prime mover of action, but only one way to clarify the validity of an action and be an effective influence on the people.

People by different practices achieve success, some cautious and some impetuous. These varying paths to success depend on whether they conform their methods to the culture of the times to achieve the advantage of the wind at their backs even if their goals are to change society. Trying to change everything at once fails since humans are not the only force on the planet, and people have differing and multiple interests. Recognizing the value of solutions that fit into existing ecosystems cannot be overly emphasized, since they do not put excessive stress on non-human support systems.

For example, oligarchs' problems with the Middle East stem significantly from energy policy, which can be changed, but the oil itself cannot be changed. Its character drives both technical solutions and political conditions. Excessive dependence on oil has resulted in less-productive lands throughout the region, exacerbating conflicts, and leaving many without a means to support themselves. These people become rootless and are then easily swayed by the mullahs.

Often, too, change has unintended consequences. For example, safety measures in automobiles in the US are greater than in the UK, where cars drive faster on more dangerous roads. But drivers are more likely to be seriously injured or killed in an accident in the US because they relax their guard and cannot regain control during an accident. Control of driverless cars cannot easily be restored by a driver who assumes that the car will take care of itself. Airline pilots cannot recover quickly during emergencies if they are habituated to autopilot. This is true for many measures that give us a false sense of security. Our attention flags, and we do not foresee danger. If we only look at the results of recent experience instead of at the whole of known experience, we are less likely to foresee major changes when we come under stress.

If an oligarch governs with caution and patience, you will sometimes find that time and affairs converge on success. But if the times and affairs change toward another direction, you are ruined, because relying on conservative measures, you cannot promptly change course. An oligarch may be insufficiently flexible in accommodating change, both because you cannot deviate from your own nature, and, having always prospered by acting in one way, you cannot be persuaded that it's a good idea to work otherwise. Therefore, excessively cautious individuals or strategies, when it is time to turn adventurous, are unable to alter course. Here we see the strength of the oligarchic network as opposed to the wit and strength of any one individual. If one point of view fails due to circumstances, another leader with another set of assumptions may be more effective and rises to the situation. This was the hope of the US citizens in electing Trump.

We conclude that events are difficult to predict, change is continuous, and humanity habituated in its cultures. Since no general behavior is always better than most others, the best combination of cautious and adventurous is related to the matter at hand rather than to some fixed practice based on either morality or character. But the changes that occur daily require you to face every day anew as an opportunity and an adventure rather than hiding in your bunker hoping the world will be the same or better tomorrow.

Remember, an oligarch's friends and cohorts are there to help the system to work even if the oligarch is no longer able to hold up the world alone. This network of mutual support remains the key to oligarchic power and would benefit citizens and workers as well. Promoting any tendency or idea against cooperation and mutual aid as the dominant feature of human society, whether it be sole reliance on individual skill or competition among entrepreneurs, is disinformation and should be viewed skeptically. Those purveying such strategies do not support your long-term interests and seek to undermine the basis of your power.

Chapter XXVI: An Exhortation to Liberate Nations and Their Citizens from Marketplace Mentality

We have considered the ecosystems of politics. We have wondered whether present times are favorable for a new leader to emerge who acknowledges the interdependence of networks and the value of cooperation. We have weighed whether current conditions might present an opportunity for far-sighted oligarchs to introduce an order based on mutual aid. Such an order would honor them individually and collectively, improving the well-being of the people as well as helping to stabilize politics and the biosphere. It appears that so many things favor such changes that there is no time like the present to act.

The current situation seems ideal for creating an alternative to the competitive financialization of so many human activities that should be freed from the marketplace mentality such as education, delivery of medical care, elections, legislating, and economic opportunity. Institutions in the developed world have been debased by finance, fetishizing human relations and corrupting our environment. A new generation of oligarchs can now make apparent how the current situation may be changed and the people liberated from the appetites of finance. It may also turn out that financial matters themselves will benefit from being applied in appropriate situations, rather than treating every interaction as commercial.

Such a spark has been shown by one oligarch, who makes us think that he intends to support our survival as a species by creating technologies for broad use that do not further degrade the biosphere. We hope that other oligarchs will not reject him entirely in spite of their differing values. We hope they will not regress behind a wall of short-term self-interest, although stress tends to drive short-term behaviors. Instead world leaders might use their networks to support the direction of this new oligarch, since it is to the majority's benefit in the long run to replace fossil fuels and eschew the marketplace model in those activities listed above. The majority of the people worldwide are ready and willing to follow this banner, if he will raise it in conjunction with others of like mind, so that thoughtful and powerful people everywhere can pursue sustainable policies, invention, and productivity.

We do not now see any others in whom we can place more optimism. Your illustrious endeavors with their forward-looking investments, your awareness of the interactions of the many components of indigenous life, and your willingness to be as transparent as possible with the people about opportunities for human improvement reduce how much our activities compromise the integrity of our surroundings. Such advances will be aided by recalling the actions and lives of the leaders we have discussed. Although they were great, they were human, and none of them had more opportunity than the present offers. Their situation was not more supportive of them than yours of you.

Those of us—activists, intellectuals, artists, and organizers—working for change seek environmental justice, recognizing the imbalances in society, as well as the biosphere. Change is happening all the time and is accelerating in recent years. If we don't change ourselves, we become victims of change instead of benefiting from it or at least accommodating our cultures to it. As with this book, we take the best of what is given, common, well-considered, and constant in our surroundings and, while maintaining its value, add what is changing to improve our understanding and to benefit the majority as well as creating opportunity for adventurous individuals. This book has hardly needed to invent and invents throughout. This recycling strategy combines with this book's subject matter, to illustrate how both specialized and interdisciplinary knowledge support our lives.

Many progressive endeavors have failed. Financial interests labor to make it appear that the marketplace if left to itself would be more propitious than regulatory intervention. But in fact, markets are inherently regulated and well organized. The market stalls are arranged in aisles. They may be regulated by participants for their own benefit, as in the oxymoronic free market, or they may be regulated by a combination of market participants and governments seeking to benefit the people, as well as the primary participants. These latter are the most successful marketplaces. Even a cursory look at past financial cycles supports this perspective. When regulation that accommodates both the needs of the people and leading market participants is withdrawn, mistakes are costlier, and private losses are charged to the public treasury. This occurs because ultimately the markets are a reflection of and in some cases a driver of economies. The arcane contention that the markets are always right is true only after the fact and does not imply that markets should lead policy, because markets are unpredictable. The logical fallacy, *post hoc ergo propter hoc*, applies to this argument. Finally, well-regulated markets increase demand, since low demand remains the key problem in highly unequal economies. Even if government regulation makes errors, those errors are not as costly to the society as those errors foisted on the people by leading market participants playing a winner-take-all game.

If too many parts of society operate on a marketplace model, even those that are actually active markets will not benefit because the other parts of the economy will drag them down too. We have seen this suppressed growth and financial repression in developed nation economies since the great recession of 2007. Components such as education and health care suffer because education is not about discovering the price for a degree, but about enhancing the benefits to students. Medical care seeks to improve the health and well-being of patients and to prevent illness, rather than to maximize the profit of antibiotics or surgery. In addition, healthy people contribute to society and thereby benefit the largest number of people, including pharmaceutical executives.

When marketplace mentality is applied to education, university boards comprised of developers benefit from building projects, but students suffer from higher costs, scholastic standardization, and less attention paid to their education. When the marketplace model is applied to medicine, the health of the people suffers so that in the US, where the market dominates medical practice, lifespans are shorter, infant mortality is higher, productivity suffers from poor nutrition, and the increase in medical technology for the few is not significantly better than in countries where all citizens' health is paid for by a single-payer system, and the market, while not ignored, isn't primary.

In a marketplace of political candidates where oligarchs throw billions at legislators to control them, the people no longer support the government and think government is the problem. The people think it is government's fault that governance is arrogant. In actuality, misdirected oligarchs both in and out of government fail to understand their long-term self-interest and only consider getting laws passed to benefit their bottom line. This is true in the courts and the executive as well as in the legislatures, since all three branches of US government must now pay for their offices and cannot spend time on the people's business. The body politic falls ill and suffers when leaders operate mainly to benefit their factions.

The opportunity, therefore, should not to be allowed to pass to let the media at last see leaders appear who can help the world rebalance. You cannot underestimate the support that you would receive in all those jurisdictions that have suffered from financialization and high-level corruption. What door would remain closed? And of course, you will remain modest in your demands.

Who would refuse to support clean transportation and energy at competitive prices, since energy must be cost effective for all to thrive? What resentment, besides certain vested interests that we have carefully noted, would inhibit progress, when not only the biosphere would benefit, but also when an environmental model of society prioritizes balance?

Such a model would encourage each component of our society to manifest itself both on its own terms and together. This model of diversity implies that all components will not thrive under the same criteria, since each has unique features that make it vital for medicine to be managed medically, education educationally, and politics politically rather than treating all human interactions as driven by a marketplace abstraction.

Let, therefore, your illustrious firms take up this charge with such courage and hope as all just enterprises are undertaken, so that under its standard our world may be moved back from the brink. And under your auspices may be realized that saying of Wordsworth:

> Come forth into the light of things,
>   Let Nature be your Teacher.

NOTE ON DEFINITIONS

This book refocuses the conversation about governance from form to operations. Rather than giving the reader a complete definition of oligarch or oligarchy at the beginning, we have preferred to build the identities of the oligarch, oligarchy, and their networks from relevant concepts and contemporary examples, because oligarchic control reaches deeper into our lives through the rule of a few and is more central to managing society than any particular form of government. The notion promulgated by some that an oligarch can be separated from the network, concepts, and functions that support that oligarch appears naïve and purposely fictional, since the forms and institutions of every society have been and continue to be dominated by those highly productive individuals, who, regardless of actual wealth, dominate human interaction and now even the biosphere. Further the reader's expectation of matching each example to an *a priori* definition defeats the purpose of functional definition. Finally, modern thought, being probabilistic, supports this kind of abductive logic, which will be more useful than trying to squeeze the entire world of power into a few phrases or only defining it as the province of an individual. Yet there will be those who feel at sea in the modern world and lean toward a more circumscribable ecosystem, and so we provide space for your definition now that you've read the book: oligarch, n, ol-i-garch, (/ˈäləˌgärk/) . . ..

© The Author(s) 2018
J. Sherry, *The Oligarch*, DOI 10.1007/978-3-319-62169-2

GPSR Compliance

The European Union's (EU) General Product Safety Regulation (GPSR) is a set of rules that requires consumer products to be safe and our obligations to ensure this.

If you have any concerns about our products, you can contact us on

ProductSafety@springernature.com

In case Publisher is established outside the EU, the EU authorized representative is:

Springer Nature Customer Service Center GmbH
Europaplatz 3
69115 Heidelberg, Germany

www.ingramcontent.com/pod-product-compliance
Ingram Content Group UK Ltd.
Pitfield, Milton Keynes, MK11 3LW, UK
UKHW021324180426
11947UKWH00017B/1422